Log Ca
IMPROV

QUILTS WITH A TWIST ON TRADITION

Landauer Publishing

Mary M. Hogan

MW00564071

LOG CABIN IMPROV

Landauer Publishing, www.landauerpub.com,
is an imprint of Fox Chapel Publishing Company, Inc.

Copyright © 2022 by Mary M. Hogan and
Fox Chapel Publishing Company, Inc.,
903 Square Street, Mount Joy, PA 17552.

Project Team
Managing Editor: Gretchen Bacon
Acquisitions Editor: Amelia Johanson
Editors: Amy Deputato, Christa Oestreich
Copy Editor: Sherry Vitolo
Designer: Mary Ann Kahn
Indexer: Jay Kreider
Proofreader: Kurt Conley

ISBN 978-1-947163-89-8

Library of Congress Control Number: 2021948606

We are always looking for talented authors.
To submit an idea, please send a brief inquiry to
acquisitions@foxchapelpublishing.com.

Printed in China
25 24 23 22   2 4 6 8 10 9 7 5 3 1

CONTENTS

IMPROV WITH A PURPOSE

Definitions of improvisation include "doing something spontaneously and without planning," "making it up as you go," and "using what is available." I love quilting this way. For me, improvisation is a type of play. I don't worry much while I enjoy the process, and I don't take myself too seriously. I usually begin with a pile of fabric and a vague idea. I start sewing, come up with some guidelines, and then change them if they no longer work. However, I always keep in mind that my purpose is to complete a quilt.

Most guides to improv quilting suggest developing a composition by placing improv pieces on a design wall, moving the pieces around, adding new pieces, moving them around, adding new pieces, and so forth. While this is a promising way to create a design, it can also be frustrating and difficult, especially for newcomers to improvisation. This book takes a different approach to improv: we'll use the log cabin block as a foundation for improvisation, which will make it easy to get started and help ensure that you can finish your quilts.

This book is written for quilters who are interested in improvisation yet stymied by the large blank canvas implied by the process and the difficulty one can encounter in finishing an improv quilt. Instead of an empty design wall on which to design a quilt, log cabin blocks provide a structure within which improv takes place. Rather than starting with an unknown (and perhaps unreachable) outcome, you will start with the knowledge that by making improv log cabins, you can easily create a quilt. Within the log cabin block structure, and with just a bit of planning, you can explore a variety of improv techniques while remaining confident that you will achieve your desired result: a finished quilt.

Chapter 1

GETTING STARTED

Improv is very simply making something out of what you have on hand and without planning. With log cabin quilts specifically, it's just a matter of cutting some fabric and sewing then cutting what you've sewn. Or cut more pieces and sew some more. Add some borders around a center piece and call it a log cabin.

When I improvise, I don't worry much about the end result. Instead, I enjoy the process. I love to quilt. I love to sew. This is the spirit that I'd very much like to communicate to everyone reading this book: improv is all about having fun.

Let's begin with the basics. We'll start with how I consider a design, how I select fabrics, what tools I favor, the basic log cabin varieties, and my general instructions for joining pieces.

IMPROV DESIGN CONSIDERATIONS

For me, design usually happens sometime after I start sewing. My process goes something like this: I start making log cabin (or other) blocks from a pile of fabric. After I've made a few "somethings," I start thinking about what I am doing, where I am going, what am I enjoying most, and what fabrics are at hand, and then I come up with a rough plan. Sometimes at this point I entirely abandon what I've been doing and go in another direction completely.

One of the first things to consider is the mood of the quilt. Do you want the quilt to be wild and wacky or quiet and orderly? Do you want to use every color in the rainbow or a specific color theme? I often choose wild and wacky by adding a lot of crooked and wonky logs and using many different fabrics and colors, but you may prefer a more coordinated palette of colors and fabrics—perhaps with an oddball or "zinger" fabric to add some interest. You'll find all these variations in this book.

For improv quilts, it is also important to consider both variety and unity. Variety is fun and exciting, but the blocks in a quilt should look like they belong together. In the end, the quilt should make sense instead of being simply a collection of disparate elements. The use of the log cabin block itself offers one aspect of unity in these quilts. Repeating a fabric, color, shape, or motif in some or all the blocks also can help unify a quilt. The projects in this book show examples of what produces unity and variety, and you can use these principles in your own projects.

Examples of Unifying Elements

- Using the same fabric and shape at the center, as in Big Orange Boxes (page 58), Courthouse Steps (page 94), and Beginner's Log Cabin (page 50).
- Using a limited number of colors, as in Two-Color Log Cabin (page 62), Red, Gray, and Black Log Cabin (page 66), and Red, White, and Blue (page 70).
- Using a common shape within blocks, as in Stack, Slash, Shuffle, and Sew (page 120).
- Using skinny string joins and a similar fabric style, as in Wonky Log Cabin with Lines (page 78).

Examples of Adding Variety

- Using different fabrics, colors, and color values (darkness or lightness).
- Altering the angles and orientation of the logs.
- Incorporating some of the improv techniques introduced in Chapter 2 (page 14).
- Including some surprises (what others might call "accents"), for example, bits of a strikingly different color, something very dark where everything else is light, or a skinny or pieced string.

The block centers are a unifying element in Big Orange Boxes.

Notice the common shape used within the blocks of Stack, Slash, Shuffle, and Sew.

The skinny strings and selvage strings in some blocks adds variety.

Varying the angles and shapes of the logs adds contrast and interest.

Leftover fat quarters in all colors and prints are great for improv quilts.

WHAT YOU'LL NEED

The usual sewing and quilting supplies are sufficient for the techniques and projects in this book. In this section, I briefly discuss what you need to get started.

Fabrics and Other Materials

When I first began quilting, I used inexpensive fabrics. I did not see or feel the difference between craft-store fabrics and quilt-store fabrics. In fact, when I started quilting, I did not even know about quilt stores! Over time, I've come to appreciate the benefit of quality fabrics; they feel better, last longer, and are a pleasure to work with. Use quilt-store quality fabrics if you can, as they will stand the test of time.

Log cabin blocks are a great way to use what you have in your scrap bin, but don't be limited by your scrap bin. I sometimes start with fabric from an abandoned project or quilt kit. Surplus fabric from a completed project or a selection of eight to twelve fat quarters has served as a starting point for a scrappy log cabin quilt. I love adding fabrics to any project, so I dig into my scrap bin to find pieces to add to the main fabrics. Consider using orphan blocks— finished or partially made blocks that never made it into a quilt. Their shapes can add interest to your log cabin blocks.

MATERIAL SUGGESTIONS FOR LOG CABIN IMPROV

• Leftover fat quarters

• Surplus fabric from projects

• Fabric from an abandoned project

• Unused quilt kits

• Orphan (unused) blocks

• Selvages

• Unusual materials: trim, lace, nylon zippers

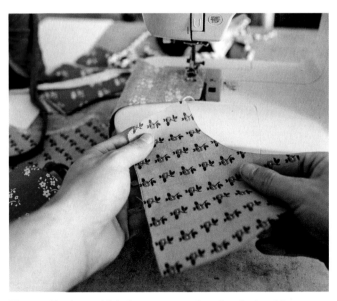

Unusually shaped fabric scraps can inspire design ideas.

Cutting Tools and Rulers

Rotary cutters make cutting fabric easy and quick. I prefer rotary cutters with 45mm or 60mm blades, rather than smaller rotary cutters, for this kind of work. Make sure the blade is sharp, and remember to always close the cutter immediately after use. When using a rotary blade, a cutting mat protects your work surface and your blade, and many have grid lines so that you can measure as you cut. Purchase a good pair of fabric scissors for cutting matching curves, trimming blocks, and snipping threads. You should also have a seam ripper handy for those times when things do not go as planned.

I suggest using a long ruler, such as 6½″ (16.5cm) x 24″ (61cm), for cutting width of fabric (WOF) strips and a shorter ruler, such as 3″ (7.6cm) x 12″ (30.5cm), for trimming blocks as you sew. Square rulers are ideal for trimming the final blocks but are not absolutely necessary. I like to use a rotating mat for trimming blocks, or use a small mat and turn it as you trim.

Sewing-Station Supplies

A sewing machine with a straight stitch is all that you really need, although I do recommend using a zigzag stitch for sewing selvages. Use whatever type of thread works well in your machine. I set up a pressing station (a small iron and pressing mat) and a cutting station (a cutting mat and small ruler) close to my sewing machine. This makes it convenient to press after sewing each seam and to trim the edge before adding a new log. Use starch or a starch alternative (I like Best Press™) to flatten the seams well. When pressing completed blocks, I use a regular ironing board and iron.

Foundations

A foundation is simply a piece of paper or fabric upon which the block is made. A foundation offers support and acts as a pattern. If using a paper foundation, such as parchment paper, you remove the foundation after making the block; if using non-woven interfacing or a similar material, you do not remove the foundation. Foundations are recommended for irregularly shaped block centers, such as circle log cabin blocks, and are used for only a few techniques and projects in this book.

TIP

Working with scrappy blocks offers a great opportunity to use up bobbins with leftover threads—just keep in mind that dark threads may show through light fabrics.

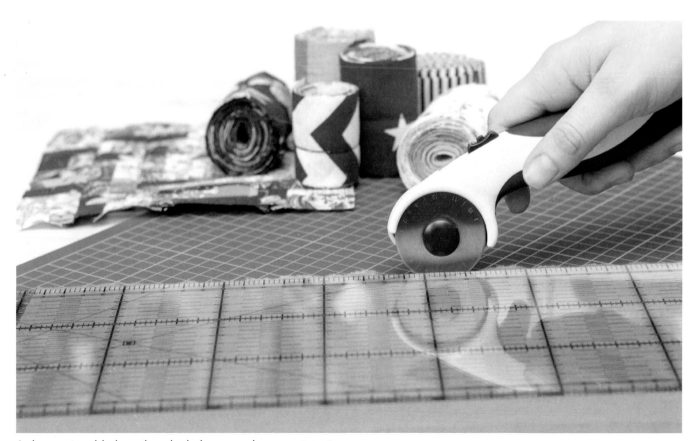

A sharp rotary blade and a ruler help you make accurate cuts.

LOG CABIN BLOCK BASICS

If you've never made log cabin blocks, the basic blocks and several variations are introduced here, along with an overview of how they are made.

The Log Cabin Block Family

A log cabin block has a few basic components: the center, logs, and joins, explained here. Traditionally, the basic log cabin block has a *center* square, also called the *starting piece* (half log cabin blocks have a corner starting piece). You then add (or *join*) strips of fabric (*logs*) in varying ways to make different blocks. Varying these basic components produces different log cabin blocks, and the placement and rotation of these blocks allows for many different quilt designs, making log cabin blocks a longtime quilting favorite. To make improv log cabin blocks, the maker works with these same basic components: centers, logs, and joins.

In addition to the usual log cabin blocks, I include some less common variations in this book. Here are examples of the main blocks in the log cabin family.

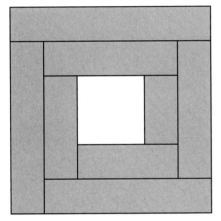

Log cabin blocks share certain features: Centers, logs, and joins. In this diagram the *center* is white and the *logs*, fabric strips added around the center, are gray, and *joins*, the seams where the logs are added, are black.

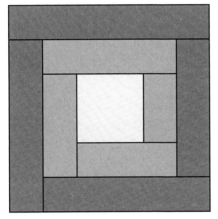

The traditional log cabin block starts with a square center. Logs are added one at a time, either clockwise or counterclockwise, around the center square. After one round is complete, a second round is added, and so on.

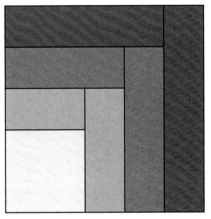

The half log cabin block starts with a corner square. A log is added to one side of the square and then to the adjacent side. More logs are added, alternating between the two sides.

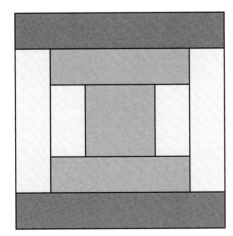

The courthouse steps block starts with a center square. Logs are added to opposite sides, then to the other two sides.

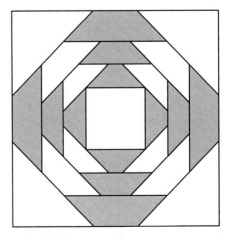

The pineapple block starts with a center square. Logs are added to four sides, then logs are added *diagonally* to the corners and trimmed. This pattern continues until the block is the desired size.

General Instructions

The log cabin is an ideal block for improvisation. One of my guiding principles for improv is to have fun! Be creative and joyful as you make each block and the finished project. It is your quilt, so do what makes you happy. As long as you carefully cut each block to the same size, the quilt will fit together. The following tips provide some guidance for your work.

Technical Tips

Improvisation does not mean shoddy workmanship! Your work will show best with well-made blocks. I developed these general technical tips while working on the projects in this book.

- The basic process for adding fabric is:
  1. Add a log.
  2. Press away from the center.
  3. Turn the block 90 degrees to the left.
  4. Trim before adding the next log.
  5. Repeat.
- Shorten the usual stitch length slightly when adding logs; this limits unraveling when you trim the edges.
- Before adding a new log, be sure to press well and trim the edge straight (unless you are intentionally making a curved join).
- Use starch or a starch alternative when pressing to keep the block flat as you work.
- Press all seams away from the center unless it is a special circumstance, such as pieced logs.
- Foundations are useful for supporting odd-shaped centers and keeping blocks flat.
- A square ruler will help you accurately trim the finished blocks.

Use press lines as a guide to correct crooked seams.

Tips for Flat Blocks

Sometimes my blocks do not lie flat. If you encounter the same issue, consider the following tips:

- Use a walking foot.
- Iron well on a flat surface. Use starch or a starch alternative and press from both the back side and the front side.
- Unless you want a curved join, make sure that each seam is straight and be sure to trim the edge straight before adding a new log.
- Correct crooked seams immediately after pressing. Use press lines as a guide (see photo above).
- Use a paper foundation, especially for unusual center shapes (see the following section on foundations).

Using Foundations

I've included information about using foundations here although it is a general quilting technique, not an improv-specific technique. As previously mentioned, a foundation helps keep the block flat and acts as a pattern. Use a lightweight paper foundation, such as parchment paper, or a lightweight non-woven interfacing.

To use, start with a slightly oversized foundation, say 11″ (27.9cm) square for a 10½″ (26.7cm) square unfinished block; you will trim the block to size later. Pin the starting piece (center) onto the foundation and add logs around the center. After adding each log, fold the foundation out of the way, using a seam ripper to loosen stitches when necessary. Use a ruler and a rotary cutter or scissors to trim any excess fabric underneath the new log. Press away from the center before adding the next log.

Once you've covered the foundation, stay-stitch near the edge of the block to limit distortion from the bias edge of the logs. Place a square ruler on the block and mark the cutting line around the ruler. Sew a straight stitch about ⅛″ (3mm) to the left of the line and trim to the correct size.

Use foundations for irregularly shaped block centers.

Fold the foundation out of the way after adding the log.

Before the excess fabric is trimmed.

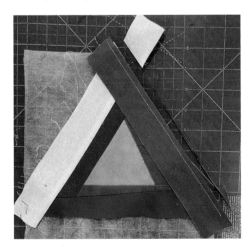

After the excess fabric has been trimmed away, the block is ready for the next log.

The finished block has been trimmed square and stay stitched at the edges

Chapter 2

IMPROVISATION TECHNIQUES

There are many ways to approach improvisation. With the aim of creating a completed log cabin quilt, the focus here is on selected improv techniques—those that can be used easily within the log cabin block format. I present a range of different techniques in this chapter, so pick and choose what you want to use. There is neither a need nor any particular benefit to using everything—these are just options.

I consider improv an opportunity for what I call "continuous creativity." Decisions are constantly being made as a quilt is made. It is my hope that you will use these ideas to produce your own improv log cabin blocks and quilts. No two projects will ever be the same, as each quilter has a unique collection of fabric and preference for certain techniques and will use what is most appealing to them.

I suggest at least scanning these improv techniques before starting a project. However, if you want to jump right in, I recommend starting with Beginner's Log Cabin Improv (page 50) or Scrappy Log Cabin with White Centers (page 54). But it's up to you! It's your time, your fabric, your quilt. Find what makes you happy and do it.

STRING SETS

To make string sets (some quilters call these *strata*), you sew together a variety of strips, cut them into straight or angled logs, and add them to blocks. When making each string set, press after adding each new strip of fabric. It's good to mix the types of fabric and widths of the strips used in each string set. Sewing rotary cut strips is straightforward; cut the strips with scissors so that the cut lines are not perfectly straight and add some interest. After sewing, press all seams to one side.

For some strips, try cutting with scissors. This leads to interesting wobbly sewing lines. I love the way these look and I've included a few tips that I developed.

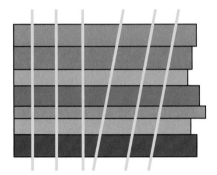

Diagram shows where to cut a string set for use as straight- and angled-pieced logs.

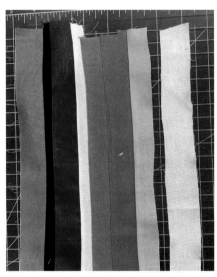

The fabrics in this string set were cut with scissors, so the edges are not perfectly straight.

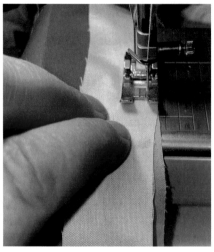

To join these slightly irregular raw edges, sew slowly and carefully, bringing the edges of the two pieces on top of each other as you sew. Use at least a ⅛" (3mm) seam width.

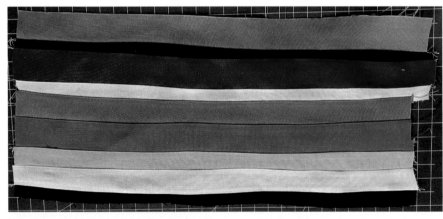

Note the wobbly joins in this string set.

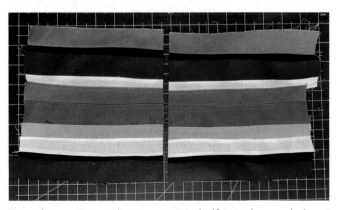

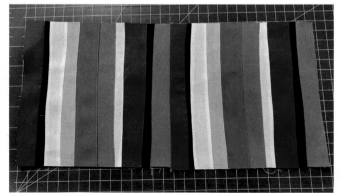

To make a string set longer, cut it in half, join the two halves into one longer string set.

SELVAGES

When I collect selvages, I cut them to at least 1½"
(3.8cm) wide to include both the selvage and some of the
fabric. I enjoy using selvages, especially in informal quilts. The
text, the images, or simply the narrow strip of white on the
selvage edges add something interesting to look at.

When deciding to use a selvage, consider sections with
interesting writing, color dots, or pictures. Place the selected
selvage *right side up* to cover the raw edge of the previous
piece by about ⅜" (1cm). Pin into place and use a zigzag or
utility zigzag to sew the selvage edge to the fabric underneath.
If using a straight stitch, sew close to the selvage edge. My
favorite stitch to use is the utility or three step zigzag stitch
shown in the diagram.

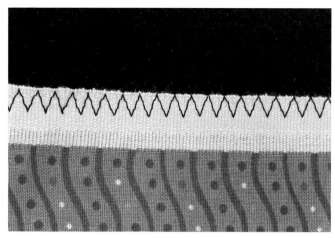

The selvage edge has been sewn right side up on top of the
previous piece.

1½" (3.8cm) is the minimum
preferred width of selvages

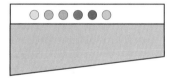

Find interesting colors or line images
on selvages.

This is the utility zigzag. You can also
use the regular zigzag.

INSERTS

Inserts are (usually) strips of fabric that are inserted within another strip or a block. In this section, I discuss regular strip inserts as well as skinny string inserts. **Note:** Also see Block Example 2 on page 67, which shows a triangle inserted within a string set.

Inserting a Strip

1. This photo shows the right side. I cut this block to add the strip of blue. I cut the blue strip longer than needed, to be safe.

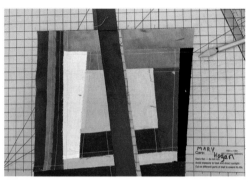

2. Sew the blue strip to one side of the gap with a ¼″ (6mm) seam allowance. Press the seam allowance toward the inserted strip. Photo shows wrong side.

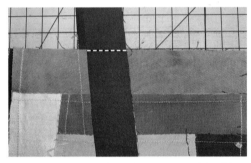

3. Draw a line as shown where the sewing of the blue insert fabric started. This identifies where sewing should begin on the other edge of the insert. Use a pencil or marker.

4. Sew the other side of the blue insert strip to the opposite side of the gap, with a ¼″ (6mm) seam. Align the edge of the block with the line on the blue insert before sewing. Press the finished seam towards the blue insert strip.

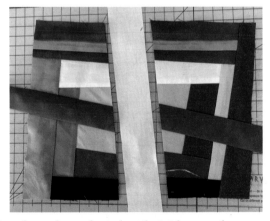

5. This photo shows the right side. Make a cut for a second insert. When adding more than one insert, complete one before starting another.

6. Add the white insert strip in the same way. Sew the insert strip to one side of the gap, draw a line across the white fabric at the beginning of the seam, then sew the other side, starting the sewing at the line. Press the seams toward the insert. To finish the inserts, the excess parts of the insert strips would be trimmed from the edges.

Skinny String Inserts

In log cabin blocks, you can use skinny strings when joining a new log or as an insert within the log itself. When making skinny string inserts (or any insert, for that matter), high contrast between the insert and the other fabrics is important; otherwise, the insert may not show up very well. After you sew a few skinny string inserts, you'll come to love them. Don't be daunted by the detailed instructions. They are here to help.

Straight Skinny String Inserts

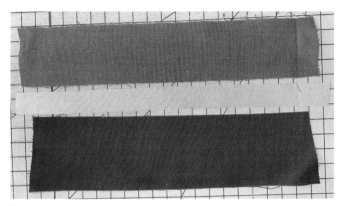

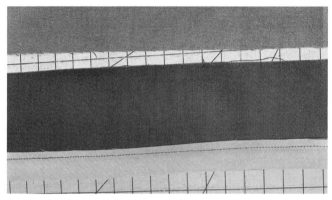

1.Select fabric for the skinny string and the two adjoining pieces. Cut all the fabric pieces larger than you think you need. In this example, the yellow piece, which will be the skinny string, is about 1″ (2.5cm) wide and cut on the straight of grain. You do not need to use a bias strip. (**Note:** After gaining experience with skinny inserts, you may feel more comfortable with narrower strips.)

2.Sew the skinny string fabric right sides together to the side of one fabric. Press the seam so that you can see the seam stitching (shown above).

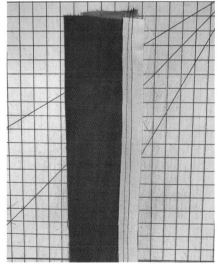

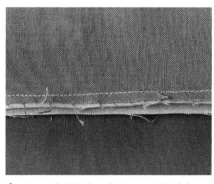

4. From the back side, press all of the seams to one side.

3. Place the other piece of fabric right side up under the previously sewn piece so that it overlaps generously. Then, using the previous seam as a guide, sew as close to the previous seam as you want. (I use my presser foot along with the previous seam to guide me.) The photo above right shows both stitching lines after the second seam has been sewn.

5. Press again from the right side.

Curved Skinny String Inserts

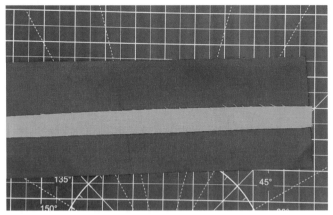 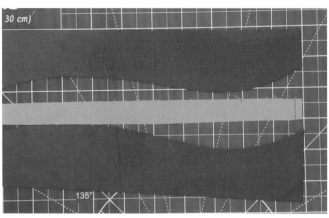

1. Select fabric for the curved skinny string and background fabric. Cut all the fabric pieces larger than you think you need. In this example, the yellow piece, which will be the skinny string, is about ¾″ (1.9cm) wide and cut on the straight of grain. You do not need to use a bias strip for gentle curves.

2. Cut a curve in the blue background fabric where you plan to insert the skinny string. Use a ⅛″ (3mm) seam allowance to sew curved edges together. Using a narrow seam helps curves lay flat. I learned this in a workshop by Dianne Hire, who also includes this tip in her 2004 book, *Quilters Playtime*.

  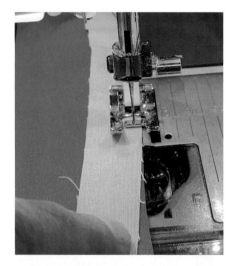

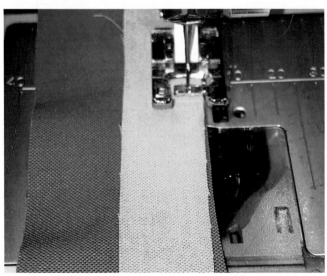 

3. Sew the skinny string fabric right sides together to the left side fabric. Use a ⅛″ (3mm) seam and, as you sew, use your left hand to bring the top fabric over the bottom fabric to match the raw edges as shown in the photos. Take your time.

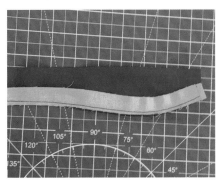 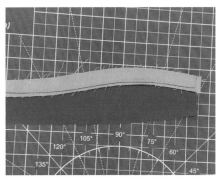 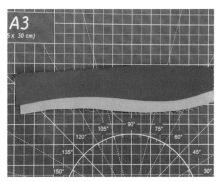

4. The photo on the left shows the seam after sewing and before pressing. Press the seam as shown in the middle photo so that you can see the seam stitching. The photo on the right shows the seam from the right side.

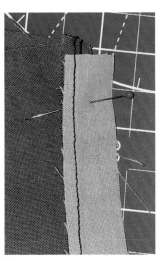   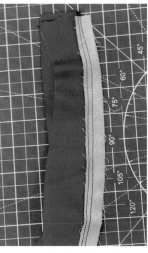

5. Place the new fabric right side up, underneath the previously sewn piece. Using the previous seam as a guide, feel the fabric *underneath* and sew as close to the seam as you want. (I use my presser foot along with the previous seam to guide me.) The photo on the far right shows both seams after the second seam is finished.

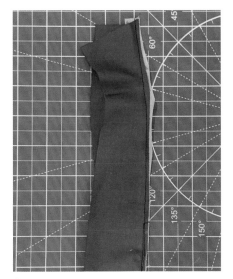 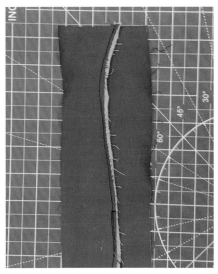 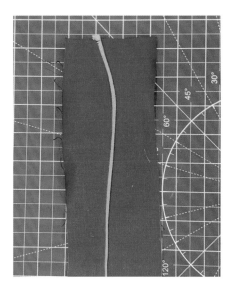

6. Trim the excess fabric with scissors.

7. From the wrong side, press all seams to the same side.

8. Press again from the right side.

9. Trim as needed to straighten the edges of the finished piece.

CUTTING AND SEWING ANGLES

Making improv quilts often leads to problematic shapes—it's not all squares, rectangles, and triangles! So it is useful to know how to deal with angles and how to move from an angle to a squared edge. It's actually quite simple, as illustrated in the following steps that explain how to cut to match angles

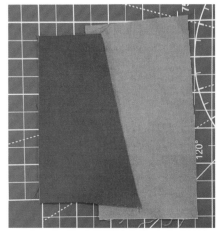

1. Find a fabric to join to the angled side of the block or fabric piece. I selected a violet piece to make the blue piece into a rectangle. Place both fabrics *right side up*, with the new fabric completely under the angled piece where the cut will be made.

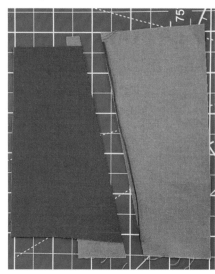

2. Cut with a ruler and rotary cutter on the line where you want the two fabrics to meet. Discard the trimmings.

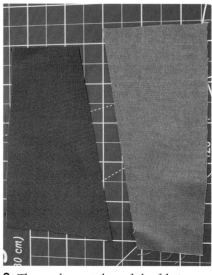

3. The angles match, and the fabric pieces are ready to sew together.

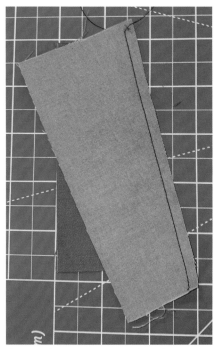

4. Sew the two pieces right sides together, with the angled raw edges lined up.

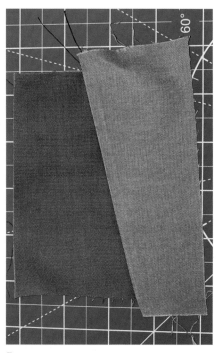

5. Open and press the piece; trim if needed.

TIP

When matching angles and curves, both fabrics should be right sides up.

CUTTING AND SEWING CURVES

To add a new fabric to a curved edge, place both fabrics with right sides overlapping where you want to sew the curve, cut the curve through both fabrics, then sew them together with a ⅛″ (3mm) seam. Press, and you're done!

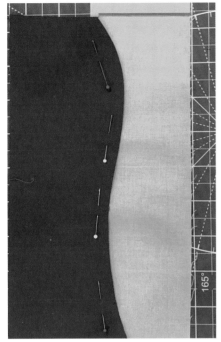

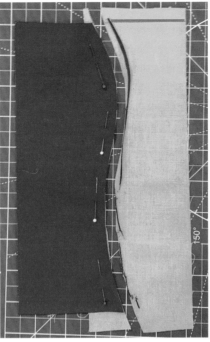

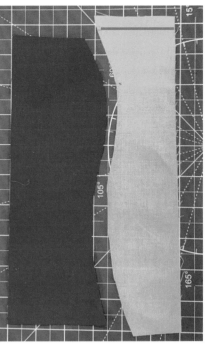

1. Find a fabric to join to the curved side of the block or fabric piece. I selected a yellow piece to sew to the curved blue piece. Place both fabrics *right side up*, with the new fabric completely under the edge of the curved piece. Draw a horizontal line (the red line in the photo) where the blue fabric aligns with the yellow fabric to mark where you will start sewing. Use pins to hold the fabrics in place for cutting and use the lines on a mat to align both pieces.

2. Cut with scissors or a rotary cutter at the place where where you want the curve.

3. Remove the pins, the fabric under the blue curved piece, and any extra bits of blue that were cut off. The fabrics are ready to sew together.

4. At the start of sewing, the two fabrics are placed right sides together. Place the top of the blue fabric at the horizontal line you drew on the yellow fabric. Pin to hold the pieces in place as you start sewing.

5. Sew the two fabric pieces together with a ⅛″ (3mm) seam.

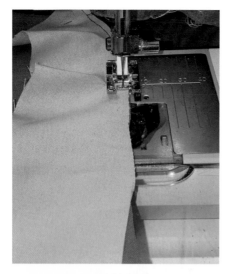 

6. Go slowly and use your left hand to place the yellow fabric on top of the blue fabric so the raw edges meet. Put the needle down when you stop sewing to avoid the fabrics shifting while you adjust the edges. The series of photos above illustrates the gradual adjustment of the fabrics as the seam is sewn.

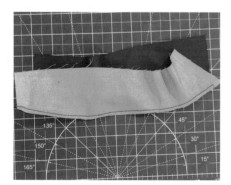 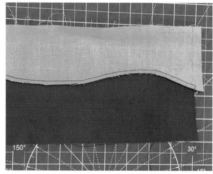 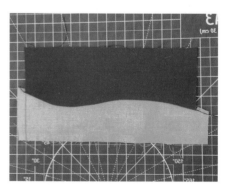

7. This photo shows the completed seam before pressing.

8. Press the seam to one side or the other. No clipping is needed for gradual curves. The photo shows the wrong side of the pieced curve.

9. Press again from the right side. The photo shows the right side of the pieced curve.

10. Trim to straighten the edges of the finished piece if needed.

IMPROV SHAPES: STACK, SLASH, SHUFFLE, AND SEW

Here's a fun way to work with improv shapes! I present some examples to get you started in this section, but you can use this technique for a wide range of shapes. The widths specified are what I used in the examples, and these sizes are large enough to make working with the pieces easy, but you can use different sizes. Going smaller can produce amazing results, but very small pieces are more fiddly to work with. It's your quilt, though, so try whatever you like! (**Note:** If you use more than two fabrics, adjust the shuffling step accordingly.)

Sawtooth Star Points

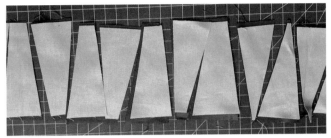

1. Stack: Cut two strips of contrasting fabric approximately 4″ (10.2cm) wide and place them *right side up* on top of each other.

2. Slash: Make angled cuts through the stacked fabric pieces. Adjust the cutting angle and position to achieve the size of the pieces and type of points (regular or flattened points) you desire.

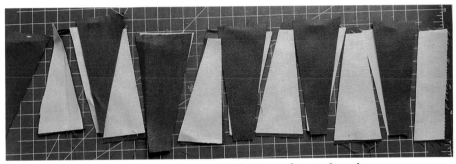

3 Shuffle: Place every other top piece to the bottom of its stack as shown.

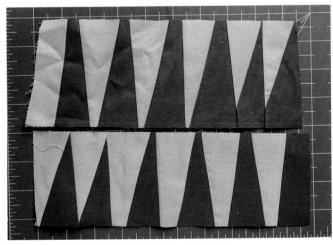

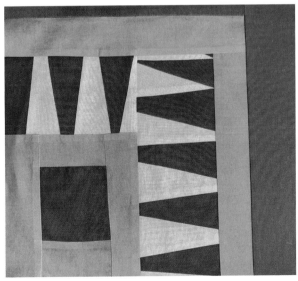

4. Sew: Sew the top layer of the stacks to each other with at least a ⅛″ (3mm) seam. Then sew the bottom layer of the stacks to each other. Each layer makes one set of sawtooth points. Trim as needed. (The finished pieces shown here were trimmed to about 3½″ [8.9cm] wide.)

5. Shown are sawtooth point logs used in a half log cabin block.

Tumblers

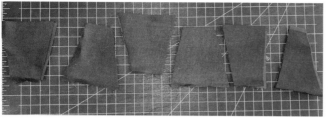 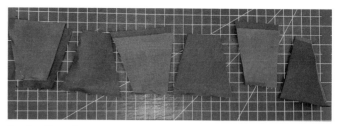

1. Stack and slash: Cut two strips of contrasting fabric approximately 3½″ (8.9cm) wide and place them *right side up* on top of each other. Make angled cuts through the stacked fabric pieces. Adjust the cutting angle and position to change the shape of the tumblers if desired.

2. Shuffle: Place every other top piece to the bottom of its stack as shown.

3. Sew: Sew the top layer of the stacks to each other with at least a ⅛″ (3mm) seam. Then sew the bottom layer of the stacks to each other. Shown is the right side of a long tumbler strip before the edges were trimmed straight.

Other Shapes

Angled Pieces

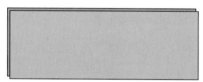

1. Stack: Layer two fabrics *right sides up.*

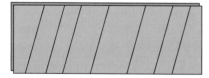

2. Slash: Cut with similar angles at irregular intervals.

3. Shuffle: Place every other top piece to the bottom of its stack as shown.

4. Sew: Sew the top layer of the stacks to each other with at least a ⅛″ (3mm) seam. Then sew the bottom layer of the stacks to each other. Shown is the top layer of angled strips, stacked. They will look similar when sewn.

Triangles

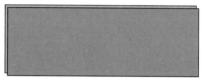

1. Stack: Layer two fabrics *right sides up.*

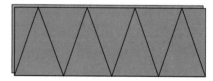

2. Slash: Cut with similar angles at irregular intervals.

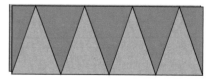

3. Shuffle: Place every other top piece to the bottom of its stack as shown.

4. Sew: Sew the top layer of the stacks to each other with at least a ⅛″ (3mm) seam. Then sew the bottom layer of the stacks to each other. Shown is the top layer of triangle strips, stacked. They will look similar when sewn.

ORPHAN BLOCKS

What are orphan blocks? Orphan blocks are blocks, parts of blocks, or any other quilt parts that you have not used. Maybe you made extra blocks you didn't include in the final quilt. Perhaps you made a block for a quilt that you later abandoned. Maybe you made some blocks as part of a workshop and did nothing further with them. Or you may have blocks with mistakes that seemed too troublesome to fix.

I love the opportunities presented by orphan blocks! When cut, they can add interesting shapes to improv blocks. I usually start by cutting some straight strips, then I change the angle and cut some more. This gives me many options to choose from.

In this finished log cabin block, the orphan block strips add unusual shapes to the logs.

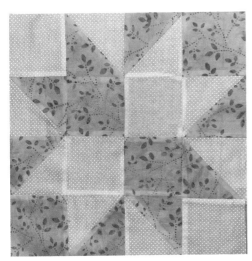
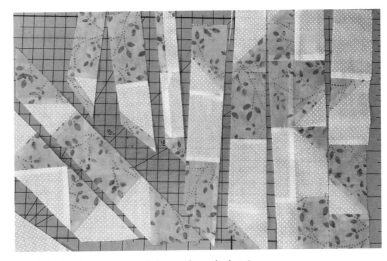

Before and after of the original block and the cut-up block. Cut some straight and angled strips.

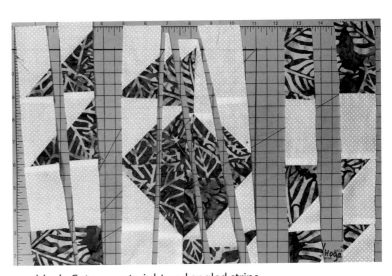

Before and after of the original block and the cut-up block. Cut some straight and angled strips.

Chapter 3

IMPROVISATION AND LOG CABINS

The quilts in this book focus on improvisation within the framework of log cabin blocks and layouts. Log cabin quilts may be as old as quilts themselves, and rare is the quilter who hasn't made one. Log cabin quilts are relatively easy because they use only rectangles and squares. At the same time, many different designs can be made from these blocks by simply varying color, value, and layouts.

Within this recognizable structure and with a little planning, you can explore a variety of improv designs and remain comfortable in the knowledge that you will ultimately end up with a familiar finished quilt.

The log cabin block organizes the improv process, ensuring a completed project. In this section, I share a variety of different approaches to help you begin your journey and inspire you to improv your own way. Log cabin blocks have centers, logs, and joins (the seams connecting the logs to the block). We'll consider the opportunities for improvisation with each of these elements.

IMPROV WITH LOG CABIN CENTERS

Traditional log cabin blocks have a square center piece, and in this section we'll explore four ways to alter log cabin centers: 1) using fussy-cut centers, 2) using varied center shapes and crooked shapes, 3) placing the starting piece in an off-center position, and 4) using constructed centers or leftover parts (such as four or nine patch blocks).

Fussy-Cut Centers

To fussy cut means to use a specific motif or specific part of a fabric. As an example, I wanted to cut a center piece from the fabric shown below that included the interesting section enclosed by the white dotted line. The finished log cabin block with this center piece is shown in the photo on the right.

The finished block using this fussy-cut center square

The entire piece of fabric

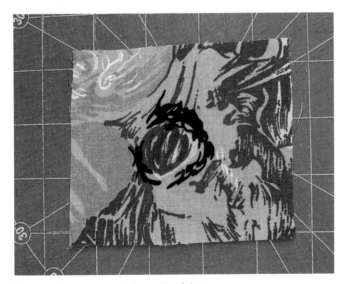

The center square cut from the fabric

Another example is the race car center pieces shown in the photo below. These were fussy cut from a larger piece of fabric. By using logs of different sizes or adding more logs to one side of the center, you can make a square log cabin block with a rectangular center.

Square log cabin blocks with fussy-cut rectangular center pieces.

Varying Center Shapes

Nearly any shape can be used to start a log cabin block. The process for making these, like other log cabin blocks, is to add pieces of fabric around the center until the block is the desired size. Even when I'm using four-sided starting pieces in the blocks of a log cabin improv quilt, I cut them freehand with scissors or a rotary cutter so they are not precisely square or a specific size. Remember—there is no right way in improv!

Quilt with Multiple Centers

The Selvage Log Cabin Quilt (page 82) demonstrates the use of many different center shapes and sizes within the same quilt.

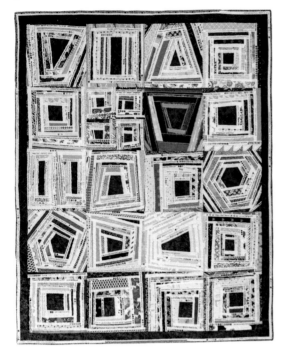

Each block in the Selvage Log Cabin Quilt has a different center.

Triangles

The quilt below was made with triangle log cabin blocks: triangle center pieces surrounded by logs. These triangles were cut in different sizes and with different angles, and many of them are tilted or rotated upside-down.

Triangles of different sizes and colors serve as center pieces for the blocks in this quilt.

Five-Sided Shapes

This baby quilt has an odd-shaped center that evolved into a five-sided shape and then extended to cover a rectangle about 36″ x 42″ (91.4 x 106.7cm). I pinned the center onto layered backing and batting, and then sewed the logs directly onto that. The logs were 2½″ (6.4cm)–wide strips of fabric. Once I reached my desired quilt size, I trimmed it and added binding.

Not only does this baby quilt have an unusual shape for a center, but the entire quilt is made from one large log cabin block.

MAKING TRIANGLE LOG CABIN BLOCKS

A triangle log cabin block starts with a rough-cut triangle pinned to a paper foundation. Join logs (or strips) around the triangle center until the foundation is covered. Trim excess fabric from underneath after adding each log.

Hexagons

I enjoy using hexagons as log cabin centers. Pin the hexagon starting piece to a foundation, add several rounds of logs, and trim any excess fabric underneath after adding each log. Once the foundation is covered, stay-stitch the edges to stabilize the block (below). The photo at the right shows a variation. Instead of continuing to add strips to make a square, several rounds of logs were added to the hexagon centers. These were appliqued to background squares.

Circles

What about using a circle as the center of a block? Yes, you can! Although it is a bit tricky, I love the way circle log cabin blocks look.

Begin by sewing small strips of fabric around the center and continue to add pieces of fabric until the foundation is covered. For step-by-step instructions on making these blocks, see the Circle Log Cabin project (page 112).

POSITIONING THE CENTER PIECE

While it would not work in a formal log cabin quilt, placing the center or starting piece off-center or rotating it can create interest in an improv quilt. For most of my log cabin improv blocks, I do not worry about positioning the starting piece right in the center. I just grab a piece of fabric to use for the center and get going!

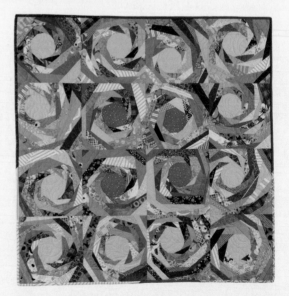

For the Circle Log Cabin Quilt on page 112, I placed each starting piece in a slightly different location, but not in the center.

The circle log cabin block has a unique swirling effect.

IMPROV WITH LOG CABIN LOGS

Pieced Logs

There are two main ways to make pieced logs: either by making and cutting up string sets or by sewing two or more pieces of fabric end to end.

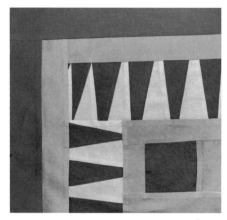

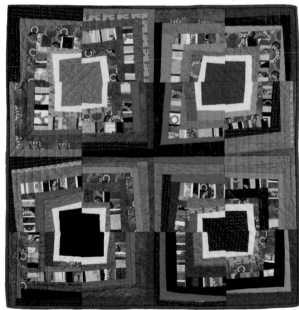

The Half Log Cabin with Pieced Logs quilt uses pieced logs cut from string sets.

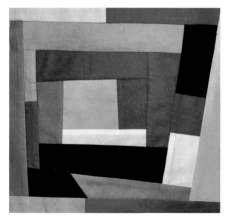

This finished block includes multiple end-to-end pieced logs.

Using String Sets

Start by making a string set (see String Sets on page 16), then cut across the string set to make a log. Sew the pieced log to the block. Press seams away from the new log, instead of away from the center, to avoid overlapping the multiple seams.

This string set can be cut to make pieced logs.

This finished half log cabin block features a pieced log cut from a string set.

Sewing Pieces End to End

Sewing same-width pieces end to end is a great way to use up smaller pieces. I usually make these pieces as I need them, using straight or diagonal seams as shown below. See also Around and Around on page 108. For that technique, I sew multiple pieces of fabric end to end before making log cabin blocks.

This photo shows fabric pieces sewn end to end with a vertical seam (top) and end to end with a diagonal seam (bottom).

Selvage Logs

Selvage strips can add a lot of interest. Look for selvages with interesting words or images. Even the plain edge of a selvage adds a nice white line to the block.

Place the selected selvage right side up so that the selvage edge is covering the raw edge by about ⅜″ (1cm). Use a zigzag or utility stitch to sew the selvage edge to the fabric underneath. Use contrasting thread for an additional design element. Also see Selvage Techniques on page 17.

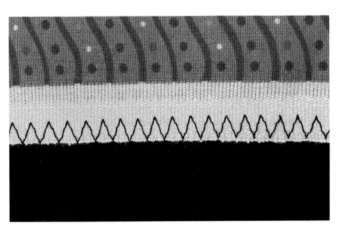

A dark zigzag stitch pops on a white selvage.

Log Inserts

Inserts in logs may include straight or curved skinny strings, as shown in the photo below. Consider other options or combinations of inserts, such as ladders and fences. See the Inserts (page 18) and Skinny String Inserts (page 19) sections for more details.

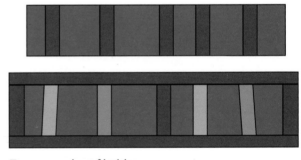

Two examples of ladders.

An example of fences.

Crooked (Angled) Logs

One of the simplest and most effective ways to improvise within the log cabin block is to use crooked or angled logs, especially if paired with a slightly irregular center piece. (See the Scrappy Log Cabin with White Centers on page 54.)

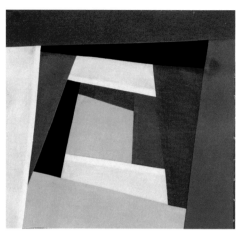

Cut angled logs from rectangles of fabric.

Join the crooked logs around the center the same way you would with straight logs.

Corners and Prairie Points

Corners

I had to invent corners when a log was not long enough, but corners can be used as an improv design element in addition to being used to solve a problem. The block pictured at right has multiple corners and one blue prairie point, which is discussed below.

1. To make corners, place a large piece of fabric right side up under the corner to be replaced. Make a cut across the corner through both the block and the new fabric.

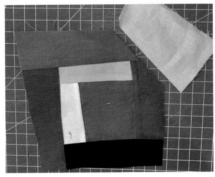

2. Discard the scraps. The yellow piece is ready to sew to the block.

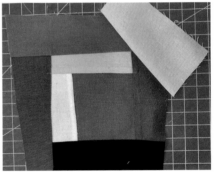

3. The new corner piece has been sewn and pressed. It will be trimmed as new logs are added.

Prairie Points

Prairie points, made from folded squares, have been used in quilting for some time, although I do not see them often in contemporary quilts. I used prairie points more than twenty-five years ago as the edging for a quilt instead of binding. In log cabin blocks, you can use them to add triangles nearly anywhere in the block.

Prairie points can be made from squares of any size. The following is a quick lesson on how to make and use them.

This block with a prairie point is from the Courthouse Steps quilt (see project on page 94).

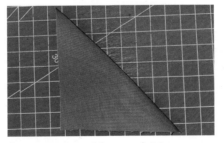

1. Start with a 4″ (10.2cm) fabric square. Fold it diagonally and finger-press.

2. Fold again and finger-press or press with an iron.

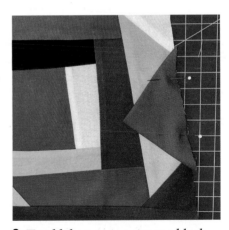

3. To add the prairie point to a block, place the prairie point with the raw edges aligned with the outside edge of the block. You will sew it into place when you add the next log. You can leave it loose or topstitch the edges.

Unusual Materials

Given the relatively casual nature of improvisational log cabin quilts, I decided to incorporate some unusual materials as a design element. I first used a zipper in a log cabin project a few years ago. I was at a quilt guild workshop, working on a project, and another member came into the classroom and passed out zippers for a different project. I decided to add mine to the quilt I was making. Why not?

I have also been saving the ties from precut fat quarters, stacks, and rolls. I added these to my collection of found and purchased trims, printed and plain ribbons, zippers, and flat cotton lace. See the Mixed Media Quilt (page 86).

After some experimentation, I found that the most satisfactory way to use these materials was to add a new log and then sew a trim onto the new log near the join. There is no particular trick or rule to adding trims—just sew it down so that it is secure and will not get caught when you are done quilting. I use two parallel lines of straight stitching for most materials.

When adding a zipper to a log, I think of it as just another trim. I usually cut off the metal parts at the top and bottom. You could also use just one side of a zipper. If you incorporate a metal zipper that still zips, be careful with the metal pieces when quilting it.

A zipper attached with zigzag stitch in a contrasting thread.

For this block, I added a purchased doily. I sewed it on by hand to keep it in place, then sewed it on more securely with machine stitching.

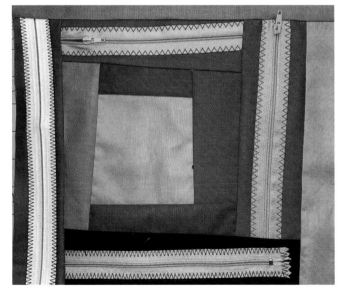

This block shows the use of four zippers. Two of them can still be unzipped.

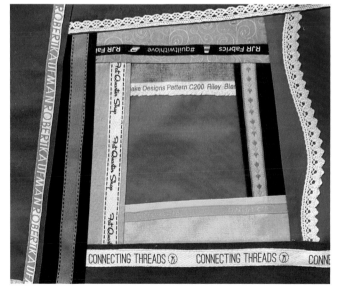

Every log in this block is decorated! One log is a selvage piece, and the rest have added trims. I used five different ties from precut fabric bundles, two ribbon trims, and two lace trims (I sewed one of them into a curve). Two lines of stitching securely attached these trims.

IMPROV WITH LOG CABIN JOINS

Altering the joins in log cabin blocks provides another opportunity for improv. In log cabin blocks, the usual join is simply the straight-stitched seam between two logs. In this section, I'll show you how to create curved joins, which is an extension of the Cutting and Sewing Curves section (page 23), and joins using contrasting skinny strings, which is an application of the techniques in the Straight and Curved Skinny String Inserts section (page 20). Another possibility is to sew seams with the wrong sides together, so seams would show on the right side.

Some of the quilt projects in this book—the Red, White, and Blue Quilt (page 70) and the Red, Gray, and Black Log Cabin Quilt (page 66)—use curved joins. One quilt—the Wonky Log Cabin with Lines Quilt (page 78)—uses contrasting joins with skinny strings for every join.

Curved Joins

To make curved log cabin joins, you'll apply the techniques in Cutting and Sewing Curves (page 23) to joins instead of simply adding a strip of fabric with a straight seam. Curved piecing is not difficult, especially when doing the easy curves shown here. With just a little practice, curved piecing will feel comfortable.

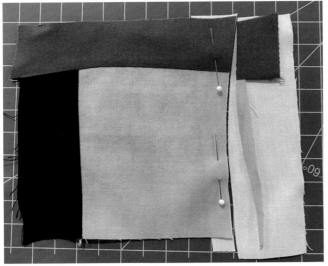

1. Place both the block and the fabric for the next log right side up and cut through both layers with an easy curve using scissors or a rotary cutter. Discard the scraps.

2. Sew the new log right sides together into place with a 1/8″ (3mm) seam allowance. Use your left hand to bring the top layer's raw edge to match the bottom layer as you sew.

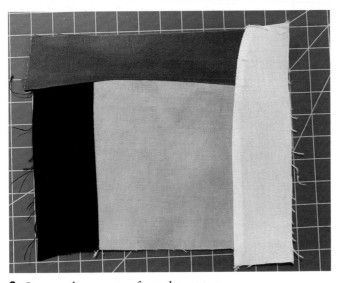

3. Open and press away from the center.

Nearly all the joins in the finished block are curved.

Skinny Strings in Log Cabin Joins

My adventures with inserting skinny strings began by playing with log cabin blocks. The following are two ways to make skinny string joins. I love how these contrasting lines show the architecture of the block.

Skinny String Option 1

With this method, the skinny string is added first to the block under construction, then the larger log piece is added.

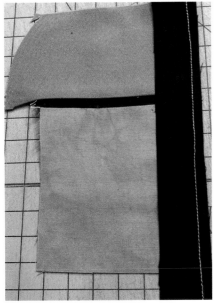

1. Add about a 1″ (2.5cm) strip of the skinny string fabric to the block with a ¼″ (6mm) seam.

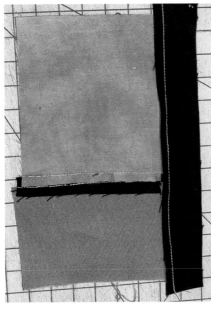

2. Press from the wrong side so you can see the seam.

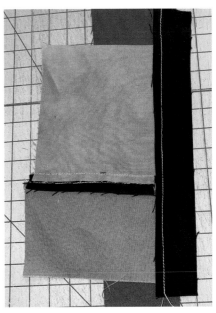

3. Place the next log right sides together under the block, leaving plenty of fabric for the overlap.

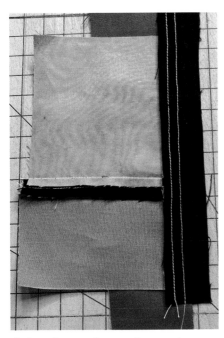

4. Sew the new log on close to the seam line of the skinny string. I used my presser foot and seam line as a guide to keep close to the seam line. The new seam is close to the previous seam.

5. Press both seams away from the center as shown from the back.

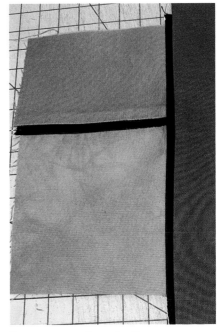

6. Press again from the front.

Option 2

With this method, you'll add the skinny string to one side of the new log before adding it to the block.

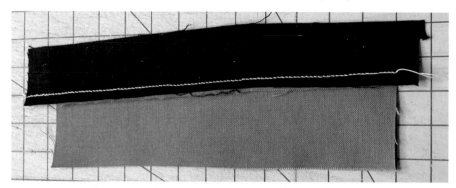

1. Sew what will be the skinny string (black fabric) to one side of the new log using the usual ¼" (6mm) seam. Press as shown so that you can see the seam line.

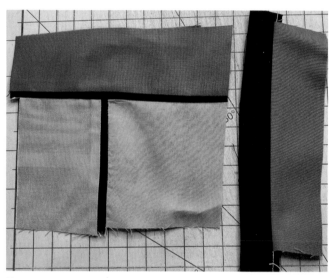

2. Trim to straighten the edge of the log cabin block.

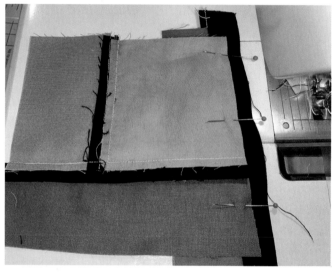

3. Place the new log with the black fabric under the block in progress as shown. Make sure the block overlaps the black skinny string enough to sew a narrow seam. Pin. Turn over so you can see the previous seam.

4. Sew close to the previous seam. Use your presser foot and the previous seam as a guide to make a skinny string. The space between the two seams will be the width of the skinny string as shown in the photo on the right.

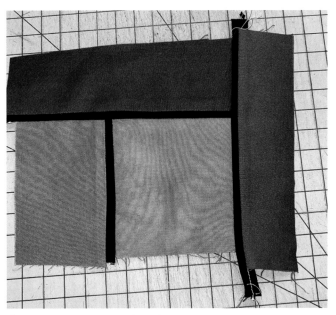

5. On the wrong side, press both seams away from the center.

6. Press again on the right side.

7. Finished blocks with skinny string joins. The block on the right uses print fabrics for the skinny string joins.

TIP

As you are constructing a block, keep in mind the number of logs needed and compare the block-in-progress to the finished size. Add wide or narrow logs, or a few extra logs, to the length or width as needed to make the block square-like. Continue adding logs until the block is somewhat larger than the size desired. Using wider logs at the outside edges makes trimming easier.

ALTERNATE LOG CABIN CONSTRUCTION METHODS

This section details alternate approaches to log cabin construction. Use these methods to make log cabin quilts that vary from the traditional log cabin look.

Around and Around

In this method, you will sew fabric strips of different lengths end-to-end into long, continuous strips. You then use these pieced strips as logs around (and around) the log cabin center. This is a great way to use up fabric scraps. For a finished project showing this technique, see the Around and Around Log Cabin Quilt (page 108).

1. Gather and/or cut strips of fabric of the same width. Cut the strips into varying lengths.

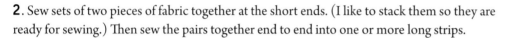

2. Sew sets of two pieces of fabric together at the short ends. (I like to stack them so they are ready for sewing.) Then sew the pairs together end to end into one or more long strips.

 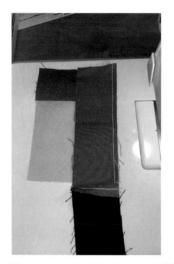 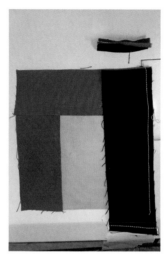 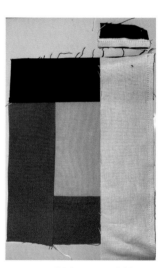

3. This is the "around and around" part. Cut a square piece of fabric for the center. Begin using a long strip of fabric to add logs around the center. This is shown in the step 3 and step 4 photos.

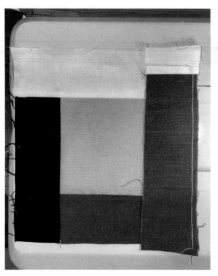 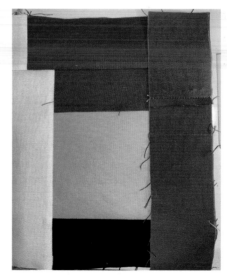

4. Continue using the long strip(s) until you've completed as many rounds as you'd like. The examples use three rounds. Trim your block to a size indicated in the chart or to whatever size you want.

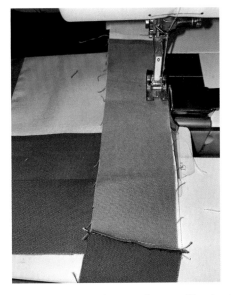
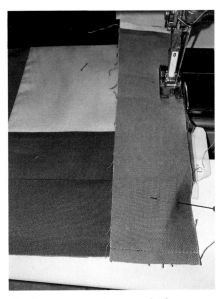

When a seam is close to the cutoff point for the log, remove the seam before sewing it in place.

Two completed blocks show how the colors pool, or come together, in various ways. These variations are what make the blocks interesting.

Table of Suggested Measurements for Around and Around Blocks

The example on the previous page uses a 3½″ (8.9cm) center square and three rounds of 2″ (5.1cm) strips, making a 12″ (30.5cm) block. The finished Around and Around project uses a 3″ (7.6cm) center and three rounds of 1½″ (3.8cm) strips, making an 8″ (20.3cm) finished block. Because 2½″ (6.4cm) strips are commonly used in contemporary quilting, I also made some blocks using those strips. This table provides suggested measurements for your convenience.

Strip width	Center square size	After three rounds, trim block to:	Finished block size
1½″ (3.8cm)	3″ (7.6cm)	8½″ (21.6cm)	8″ (20.3cm)
2″ (5.1cm)	3½″ (8.9cm)	12½″ (31.8cm)	12″ (30.5cm)
2½″ (6.4cm)	4″ (10.2cm)	15½″ (39.4cm) or 16″ (40.6cm)	15″ (38.1cm) or 15½″ (39.4cm)

Stack, Slash, Shuffle, and Sew

I introduced this method in the section on making improv shapes (page 25), and you can also use it as an alternate way to make log cabin blocks. The instructions here show a very simple example of this method for making log cabin blocks. For a more complex use of this technique, see the Stack, Slash, Shuffle, and Sew Log Cabin quilt (page 120).

Always start with squares larger than your desired finished block size. The seams and angles result in smaller finished blocks than you might imagine. In this example, the 7″ (17.8cm) squares yield 5½″ (14cm) square unfinished blocks. This example with specific measurements is shown so that you can learn and understand the technique. Make test blocks to figure out the correct sizes for any stack, slash, shuffle, and sew block you plan to use.

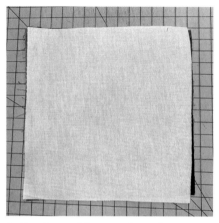

1. Stack six 7″ (17.8cm) rough cut squares. Six pieces of fabric will yield six smaller blocks.

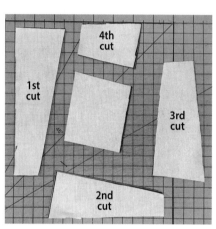

2. Slash (cut) through all layers in the order shown using a ruler and rotary cutter. Rotate the stack as needed to make the cuts. (**Note**: Using this method, the block is sewn back together in the opposite order of the cuts.)

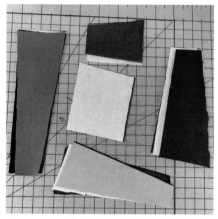

3. Shuffle by moving pieces of fabric from the top to the bottom of the pile. Move one piece from the 1st cut pile to the bottom, move two pieces from the 2nd cut pile to the bottom, and so forth.

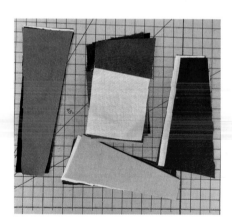

4. Sew the blocks together in the opposite order of the cuts. Sew the Cut 4 pieces to the center, then sew the Cut 3 pieces to the block, keeping the order from top to bottom, and so on.

5. After you've sewn these six blocks together, they can to be trimmed to 5½″ (14cm) squares.

Itty Bitty Piecing

Itty bitty piecing (also known as *crumb quilting*) is a good way to use small and irregular pieces of fabric. I love itty bitty piecing (even though I seem to make scraps faster than I can use them!). It is fun, but it does take a while to make a quilt this way.

There are no specific techniques to itty bitty piecing, so in this section I share how I work with small pieces. My main advice is to press and trim often. Some examples are shown below.

1. Sew together fabric pieces from your scrap pile. After making small chunks, press well and trim so you can see what you have. (I outlined some of the chunks I used in this block.)

2. Add more fabric to your chunks or sew some chunks together. Press and trim.

3. Decide on the finished block size. (I usually aim for blocks that are 6″ [15.2cm] to 12″ [30.5cm] square.)

4. Continue to add scraps, sew chunks together, and use fabric strips to make a piece large enough for your block.

In this finished itty bitty block, you can see where the chunks that I outlined in the first photo were used. I put together many of the smaller chunks to surround the center areas.

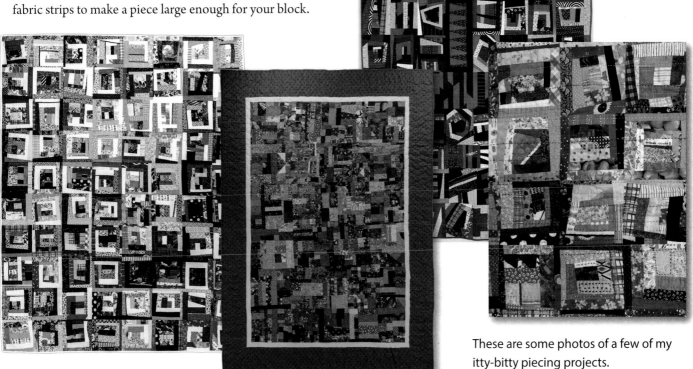

These are some photos of a few of my itty-bitty piecing projects.

Circle Log Cabin

With the circle log cabin technique, instead of having straight edges to which you continually add logs, placing fabric pieces around a circular center requires a somewhat different approach. This technique may be challenging for inexperienced sewers because it can be difficult to keep the block flat due to the many pieces of fabric added.

For these instructions, start with a 5" (12.7cm) circle and use small strips for the first round. There are very few instances in this book that use specific sizes, but, in this case, it is very helpful. If you want to use a different starting size, experiment to find what works best, especially for the first round. For a project that uses the circle log cabin technique, see the Circle Log Cabin quilt (page 112).

TIP

The key to making a circle log cabin is to carefully place, sew, and press the logs in the tricky first round. Adding a foundation after sewing the first four strips provides enough flexibility to allow you to sew the first strip to the last strip, and it helps keep the block flat. Trust me—this makes more sense when you actually do it!

1. Cut a 5" (12.7cm) circle and prepare about a dozen 1½" x 4" (3.8 x 10.2cm) strips to use in the first round, which is the trickiest round. Sew the first four strips around the circle, and then add a foundation *after* sewing the first four strips. Continue sewing the rest of the strips in the first round. See the Circle Log Cabin quilt on page 112.

2. After finishing the first round, begin to add the 2" (5.1cm) logs for the second round, continuing in the same direction around the center. While these logs are longer and wider, do not try to cover too much at one time.

3. Continue adding logs in the same way until the foundation is covered. If you used a paper foundation, remove it before sewing blocks together.

4. Mark the block at the outside edge using a square ruler, then stay-stitch (a straight line of stitching) about ⅛" (3mm) inside the marked line, and then trim. (The stay stitching helps stabilize the block, which has many seams and bias edges.)

Working with Panels

Making panel components into log cabin blocks of various sizes provides ways to enlarge panel pieces for a project. This means you can cut up panel sections, treat each section as a block center, and add logs to make blocks of various sizes.

When using panel pieces in a quilt, I recommend first mapping out the project on paper so you can decide on the final quilt size, figure out the size and number of blocks needed, and see if you have enough panel sections to create the quilt you want. If you need a few extra blocks, consider making some log cabin blocks without panel sections as centers. Borders and sashing are additional ways to help you achieve a particular size.

There is no specific way to address all types of fabric panels, but I've divided them here into three main categories: 1) single-image panels, 2) panels with multiple sections of the same size, and 3) panels with several different-sized sections. In addressing each type, I include some options of how to use them with log cabin techniques.

Single-Image Panels

With a single-panel picture as the log cabin center, logs can be added to enlarge the panel. Depending on the sizes and the number of logs added, your quilt could theoretically be almost any size. However, if you enlarge the panel too much, the center may seem out of proportion with the whole quilt. So, keep proportions in mind when deciding on the size you want for your finished quilt.

For an example, look at the quilt pictured. The panel is rectangular, and I added logs to surround the panel. The finished size is now much larger than the original panel. At this point, I felt that the proportion of the quilt parts (center and logs) was about right. The pieced logs add a lot of interest to this quilt.

Panels with Multiple Same-Sized Sections

Some panels have multiple images of the same size. Each of these panel sections can be used as the center for different log cabin blocks. Rectangular centers can become square blocks, and square centers can become rectangular blocks. This provides a lot of flexibility with design.

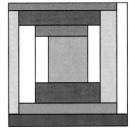

Panels with Several Different-Sized Sections

Although I used fabrics from several different panels, the quilt shown here illustrates how to use a panel with multiple varied sections. I decided to use the set of twenty-eight small panel sections as log cabin centers and to make blocks that would finish at 10″ (25.4cm) square. These blocks became the outside of the quilt. I chose two large sections to use in the center of the quilt, along with other small panel pieces. Each of these pieces in the center would require some logs to reach the correct size on their own.

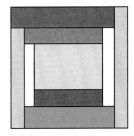

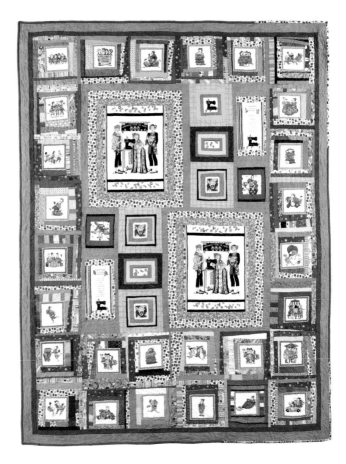

Chapter 4

LOG CABIN IMPROV PROJECTS

Now comes the best part, creating your own one-of-a-kind quilts! And each truly is one-of-a-kind. The very nature of improv brings together unique scraps, blocks, and bits and pieces in a way that's not likely to be duplicated. Even if blocks are not the same, within the log cabin framework, there's still a comfortable sense of structure once everything comes together.

I can't decide which quilt is my favorite. I love the playful, childlike impression of Stack, Slash, Shuffle, and Sew; the striking Barn Raising setting in my Two-Color Log Cabin; and the almost cartoonish effect of the Wonky Log Cabin with lines. Of course, there's a sense of the fabric in motion created by the colorful Circle Log Cabin. I just can't choose, and I sincerely hope you can't either—maybe you'll want to make them all!

The quilt projects in this chapter demonstrate some improv ideas. My hope is that you use these as a jumping-off point for your own work, instead of following them exactly.

BEGINNER'S LOG CABIN IMPROV

Learn log cabin block basics while making these scrappy blocks. There is no need to cut carefully measured strips; instead, start making blocks right away. Dig into leftover scraps and strips of fabric, then trim when the blocks are large enough. Either make a few blocks for a table runner or bag or create a whole bunch for a quilt.

Aim for variety by using many different fabrics and colors. At the same time, you can unify the quilt with a repeated fabric or motif as the center for each block. This is the simplest of improv log cabins. The block center sizes vary. The logs use many different fabrics and are different widths, but nothing complicated is going on here beyond that. This is a great way to use up some scraps.

Vital Stats

Quilt size: 60″ x 84″ (152.4 x 213.4cm)
Block size: 12″ (30.5cm) square
Thirty-five blocks, seven rows of five blocks

Quilted by **Yessant Habetz**

> ### TIP
>
> The exact seam allowance does not matter but use at least ⅛" (3mm) to secure the seam. What matters, in the end, is to trim all your blocks to the same size.

Tools and Materials

- 12½″ (31.8cm) square ruler
- Block centers: About ½ yard (45.7cm) of one fabric for block centers
- Blocks: Assorted scrap fabrics (Yardage is not provided because of the use of scrap fabrics.)
- Backing: 5⅛ yards (468.6cm):
  Cut two 92″ (233.7cm) x WOF pieces
- Binding: ⅝ yard (57.2cm):
  Cut eight 2½″ (6.4cm) x WOF strips (or make a scrappy binding)

Block Construction

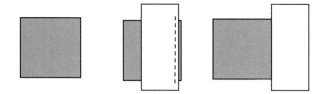 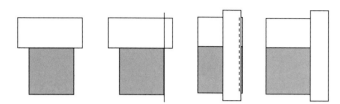

1. Start in with a 3″ to 5″ (7.6 to 12.7cm) square-like center. Select a log and join (sew) it to the right side of the center piece. Open and press the seam away from the center.

2. Rotate the block 90 degrees counterclockwise (left). Trim to straighten the edge. Join the next log. Open and press the seam away from the center.

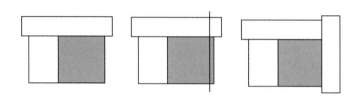 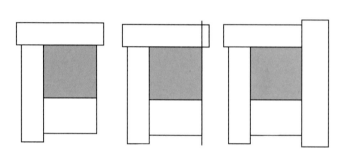

3. Rotate the block 90 degrees counterclockwise (left). Trim to straighten the edge. Join the next log (stitching lines not shown). Open and press the seam away from the center.

4. Rotate the block 90 degrees counterclockwise (left). Trim to straighten the edge. Join the next log. Open and press seam away from the center.

5. Repeat these four steps—rotate, trim, join, and press—until the block is the desired size.

6. Trim all blocks to 12½″ (31.8cm).

Make thirty-five blocks.

IMPROVISATION TIP

For this beginner quilt, try varying the colors, values, and log widths. Use many different fabrics for an exciting look.

Quilt Assembly

Arrange the blocks into seven columns of five blocks. Sew the blocks in each column together using a ¼″ (6mm) seam. Press. Sew the columns together using a ¼″ (6mm) seam. Press.

Finishing the Quilt

1. The backing piece should be at least 68″ x 92″ (172.7 x 233.7cm). Sew two 92″ (233.7cm) x WOF (42″ [106.7cm]) strips together after trimming off the selvages. Press the seam.

2. Layer the backing, batting, and quilt top together and baste. Quilt as desired.

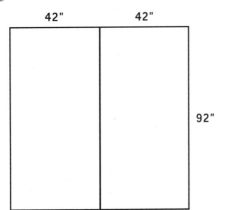

3. To bind the quilt, first sew the 2½″ (6.4cm) binding strips into one long strip using diagonal seams. Fold lengthwise with the wrong sides together and press. Match the raw edges and sew the binding to the front of the quilt. At each corner, stop stitching ¼″ (6mm) from the corner, then fold the binding up and then down as shown in the photos. Start sewing again from the top edge (dashed line) until the next corner. When you've sewn the binding around the entire quilt, fold the binding over the edge of the quilt and sew it by hand to the back side.

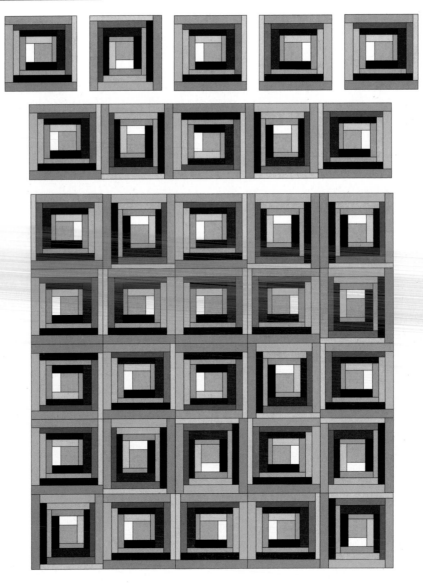

SCRAPPY LOG CABIN WITH WHITE CENTERS

This is a simple log cabin improv quilt, using white crooked square-like center pieces to create coherence within the project. This project uses a wide variety of fabrics and many of the techniques presented in this book. It's a good example of improv elements applied within the blocks.

IMPROVISATION TIPS

- Pieced logs
- Selvage logs
- Narrow logs
- Skinny strings
- Crooked or angled logs
- Zippers
- Decorative trims, lace, or ribbon

Vital Stats

Quilt size: 48″ x 60″ (122 x 152.4cm)
Block size: 12″ (30.5cm) square
Twenty blocks, five rows of four blocks

Quilted by **Yessant Habetz**

Tools and Materials

- 12½″ (31.8cm) square ruler
- Block centers: One fat quarter (18″ x 22″ [45.7 x 55.9cm]) or scraps of white fabric
- Blocks: Assorted scrap fabrics (Yardage is not provided because of the use of scrap fabrics.)
- Backing: 3¼ yards (297.2cm):
  Cut two 56″ (142.2m) x WOF (42″ [106.7cm]) pieces
- Binding: ½ yard (45.7cm):
  Cut six 2½″ (6.4cm) x WOF (42″ [106.7cm]) strips
  (or make a scrappy binding, as shown here)

Block Tour

Before the step-by-step instructions for this quilt, let's look at some of the quilt's blocks. This block tour is designed to show some improv techniques as they are used in blocks. I hope this helps you consider ways to incorporate improv in your own work.

Block 1

- All the blocks start with a square-like white center (outlined in red).
- I used four narrow navy logs for the first round (outlined in white).
- The second round (outlined in bright yellow) starts on the left with a slightly angled orange-print log. Moving clockwise, the next log is a dark green and gold fabric, slightly angled. The next log is a navy selvage piece with multicolored dots on the selvage. The last log is a flowered orange print.

Block 2

Pieced logs

Skinny string joins

- The square-like white center is outlined in red.
- The first round (outlined in white) has a dark red log, then an angled high-contrast blue-on-green polka-dot print, then a slightly angled purple print, and finally a white-on-red print.
- The second round (outlined in bright yellow) has a print on white, then an angled pea-green log, then a floral print, and finally a blue plaid print with a black skinny join.
- On the third round (outlined in bright green), the floral print has a skinny black join, then a green and white print is joined at with a selvage edge. The next log on the third round is a pieced log, cut from a string set of green and blue prints. The last log on this round is a green-on-blue print. An angled cut from the same string set is on the far left of this block at the beginning of the fourth round.

Block 3

- The square-like white center is outlined in black.
- The first round starts with the red print, then a very narrow green-on-orange print, followed by a bright orange print and then a floral print.
- Rather than a whole second round, just two logs were added (outlined in yellow): first, the light gray print, then a relatively narrow-angled pieced log (from the same string set that was used in Block 2).
- The third round (outlined in bright green) starts with a green print with a black skinny string join, then a selvage-edge log, a floral print, and another selvage-edge log. The next log, the star-like print, was attached in a different way to cover the zipper pull area, which was then cut off. You can still see a bit of the floral fabric to the left of the new log.
- The fourth round (outlined in bright yellow) starts with the light floral fabric already used, with a zipper over the join. A piece of tan twill trim with embroidered flowers is used as a log on the right.

Block Construction

1. Cut a white four-sided shape about 4″ to 5″ (10.2 to 12.7cm) that looks something like the figure shown.

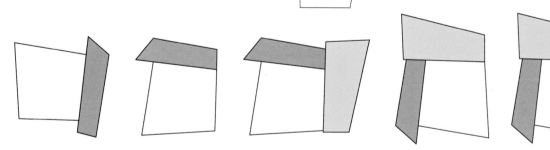

2. Join logs around the center as shown in the photo sequence from left to right: sew (join) the first log and press, then rotate the block to the left and trim, then join the next log and press. Continue in this manner until all four logs of the first round are joined and pressed.

3. Incorporate one or more of the suggested improv techniques as you work.

4. Add a variety of logs in rounds around the center until the block is about 13″ (33cm) square.

5. Trim the block to 12½″ (31.8cm) square.

Make twenty blocks.

Quilt Assembly

Arrange the blocks into five rows of four blocks. Sew the blocks in each row together using a ¼″ (6mm) seam. Press. Sew the rows together using a ¼″ (6mm) seam. Press.

Finishing the Quilt

1. The backing piece should be at least 56″ x 68″ (142.2 x 172.7cm). Sew two 56″ (142.2cm) x WOF (42″ [106.7cm]) strips together as shown after trimming off the selvages. Press the seam.

2. Layer the backing, batting, and quilt top together and baste. Quilt as desired.

3. Bind the quilt. See page 52 for binding instructions.

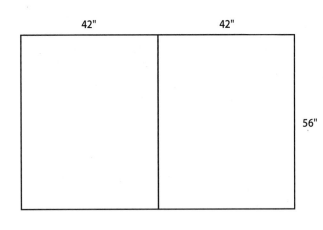

BIG ORANGE BOXES

The white with red-orange bordered centers offer a striking focal point within each block and unifies the quilt design, as the border echoes and emphasizes the block centers. The variation in size and orientation of block centers adds a sense of fun. The rest of the logs provide supporting roles. The bright prints especially add playfulness to the quilt. This quilt features a lot of angled logs.

Vital Stats

Quilt size: 68″ x 80″ (172.7 x 203.2cm)
Block size: 12″ (30.5cm) square
First border: 1″ (2.5cm)
Second border: 3″ (7.6cm)
Thirty blocks, six rows of five blocks

Quilted by **Yessant Habetz**

IMPROVISATION TIPS

• Pieced logs
• Selvage logs
• Narrow logs
• Skinny strings
• Crooked or angled logs

Tools and Materials

• 12½″ (31.8cm) square ruler
• Block centers and second border: 1½ yards (137.2cm) white fabric
• Narrow logs around centers, first border, and strips on border: At least 1 yard (91.4cm) assorted red-orange fabrics
• Rest of logs: Assorted scrap fabrics (Yardage is not provided because of the use of scrap fabrics.)
• First border: ⅜ yard (34.3cm) red-orange fabric: Cut eight 1½″ (3.8cm) x WOF (42″ [106.7cm]) strips
• Second border: ¾ yard (68.6cm) white fabric: Cut eight 3½″ (8.9cm) x WOF (42″ [106.7cm]) strips
• Backing: 5 yards (457.2cm): Cut two 88″ (223.5cm) x WOF (42″ [106.7cm]) pieces
• Binding: ⅝ yard (57.2cm) red-orange fabric: Cut eight 2½″ (6.4cm) x WOF (42″ [106.7cm]) strips

Block Construction

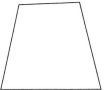

1. Cut a white four-sided shape about 4″ to 5″ (10.2 to 12.7cm), using the illustration as a guide.

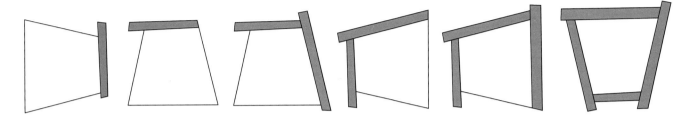

2. Cut 1″ to 1½″ (2.5 to 3.8cm) strips of assorted red-orange logs for the first round. Use a piece somewhat longer than needed to sew to the first side. Press away from the center. Rotate the block left, trim the edge straight then add the next log. Continue until the center piece is surrounded by narrow red-orange logs.

3. Following the same process, add a variety of logs in rounds until the block is about 13″ (5.1cm) square. Trim the block to 12½″ (31.8cm).

4. Repeat Steps 1–3 to make thirty blocks.

Quilt Assembly

Quilt Center

Arrange the blocks into six rows of five blocks, orienting them however you like. Sew the blocks in each row together using a ¼″ (6mm) seam. Press. Sew the rows together using a ¼″ (6mm) seam. Press.

Borders
First Border

1. Remove the selvages and sew the 1½″ (3.8cm) border strips into one long strip.

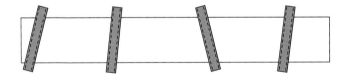

2. Measure the quilt from side to side. Cut two border sections to this length. Sew the top and bottom borders in place with a ¼″ (6mm) seam. Press away from the center.

3. Measure the length of the quilt with the top and bottom borders in place. Cut two border pieces to this length. Sew the right and left borders in place with a ¼″ (6mm) seam. Press away from the center.

Second Border

1. Remove selvages and sew the 3½″ (8.9cm) border strips into one long strip.

2. Add the red-orange strips of fabric to the border. Using the 1½″ (3.8cm) strips of fabric, fold under ¼″ (6mm) on each long edge and press.

3. Cut a piece of the folded fabric. Place wrong side down on the border piece, pin, and sew with topstitching very close to the folded edges. I sewed these on at different angles about every 6″ to 7″ (15.2 to 17.8cm).

4. Measure the quilt from side to side. Cut two border sections to this length. Sew the top and bottom borders in place with a ¼″ (6mm) seam. Press away from the center.

5. Measure the length of the quilt with the top and bottom borders on. Cut two border pieces to this length. Sew the right and left borders in place with a ¼″ (6mm) seam. *Press toward the center* instead of away from the center because of the bulk of the folded and sewn pieces.

Finishing the Quilt

1. The backing piece should be at least 76″ x 88″ (193x 223.5cm). Sew two 88″ (223.5cm) x WOF (42″ [106.7cm]) strips together as shown after trimming off the selvages. Press the seam.

2. Layer the backing, batting, and quilt top together and baste. Quilt as desired.

3. Bind the quilt. See page 52 for binding instructions.

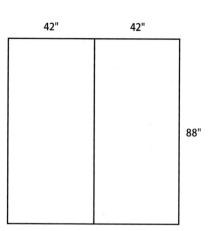

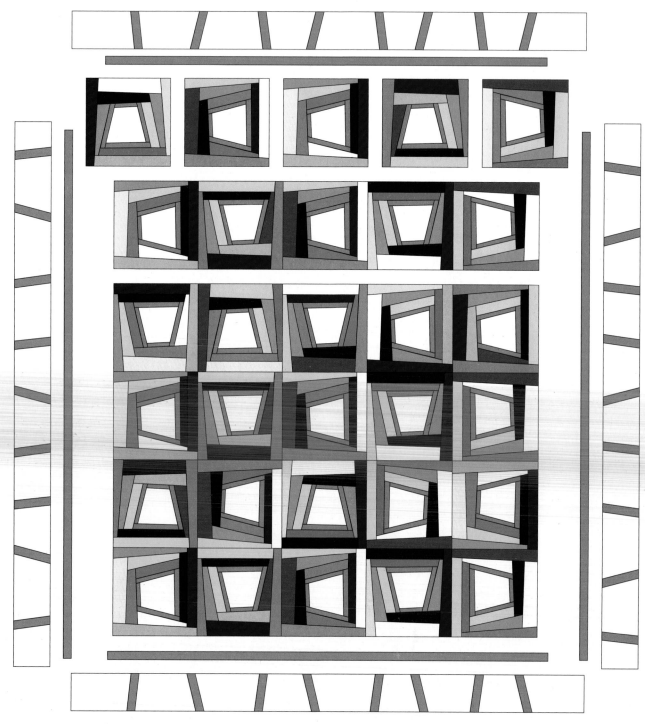

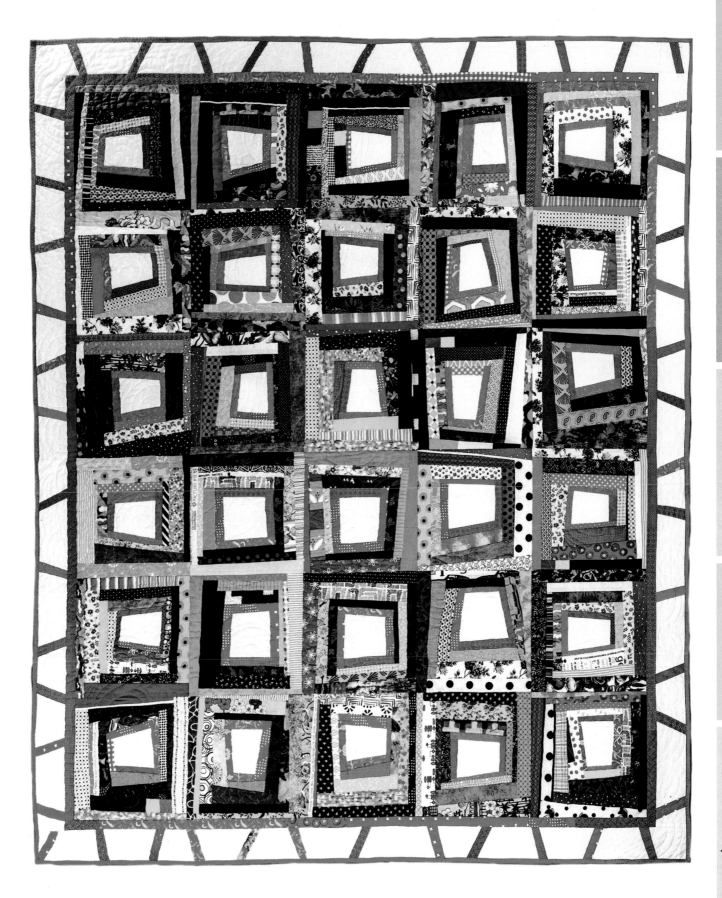

TWO-COLOR LOG CABIN

This quilt follows the tradition of making log cabin blocks with a light half and a dark half. I used the Barn Raising layout. Once you know how to make two-color blocks (whether crooked or not), you can make many log cabin designs with them.

I love the wobbly look of this quilt. Note the repetion of coral pieced logs and dark green skinny strings as well as the many different fabrics used.

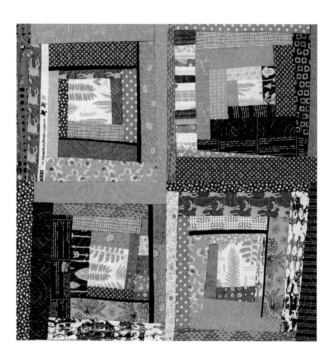

Vital Stats

Quilt size: 60" x 72" (152 x 182.9cm)
Block size: 12" (30.5cm) square
Thirty blocks, six rows of five blocks

Quilted by **Yessant Habetz**

IMPROVISATION TIPS

• Varied value and fabrics
• Angled logs
• Selvage logs
• Pieced logs
• Contrasting skinny joins

Tools and Materials

• 12½" (31.8cm) square ruler
• Block centers: ½ yard (45.7cm) light value print
• Logs: Assorted coral and turquoise fabrics or scraps, and small amounts of dark fabric for skinny string joins (Yardage is not provided because of the use of scrap fabrics.)
• Backing: 4 yards (365.8cm):
    Cut two 68" (172.cm) x WOF (42" [106.7cm]) pieces
• Binding: ⅝ yard (57.2cm):
    Cut eight 2½" (6.4cm) x WOF (42" [106.7cm]) strips
    (or make scrappy binding)

Block Construction

To make the two-color blocks, attach two light logs, then two dark logs, then repeat until the block is large enough. For the blocks in this project, I started with light logs and finished with dark logs, using four rounds for most of the blocks.

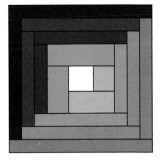

In a traditional two-color block, the center is square and the logs are straight and of a more uniform width.

This two color improv block has angles, a selvage log and several skinny string joins.

1. Start with a rough-cut square between 3″ to 4″ (7.6 to 10.2cm) for the center piece.

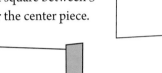

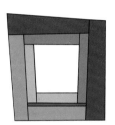

Round 2 in Progress   Completed Round 2

2. Cut the pieces for the two light logs; the first piece should be a little longer than needed. Join (sew) the first log to one side of the center piece. Press away from the center.

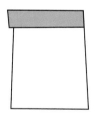

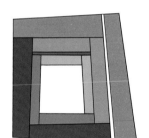

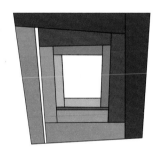

Round 3 in Progress   Completed Round 3

3. Rotate left, trim the edge straight, then add the next light log.

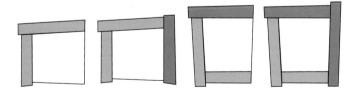

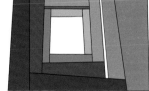

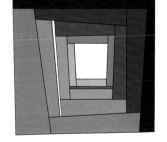

Round 4 in Progress   Completed Block

4. Rotate left, then trim the edge straight. Repeat Steps 2 and 3 to join the two dark logs.

5. Alternate between joining two light logs and two dark logs until the block is about 13″ (33cm) square. In these diagrams I'll show four rounds because many of the blocks do so.

Make thirty blocks. Trim to 12½″ (31.6cm).

Quilt Assembly

Arrange the blocks into six rows of five blocks to achieve a Barn Raising layout as shown in the quilt layout diagram. Sew the blocks in each row together using a ¼″ (6mm) seam. Press. Sew the rows together using a ¼″ (6mm) seam. Press.

Finishing the Quilt

1. The backing piece should be at least 68″ x 80″ (173 x 203cm). Sew two 68″ (173cm) x WOF (42″ [107cm]) pieces together as shown after trimming off the selvages. Press the seam.

2. Layer the backing, batting, and quilt top together and baste. Quilt as desired.

3. Bind the quilt. See page 52 for binding instructions.

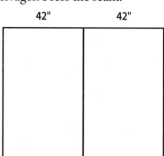

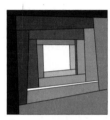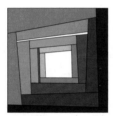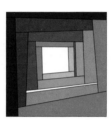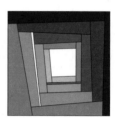

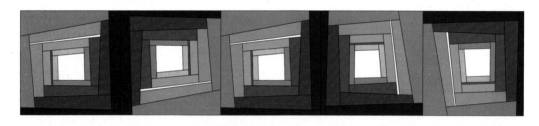

The barn raising setting is one of many classic settings for log cabin blocks. It has what looks like a center square on point surrounded by rounds of light and dark colors. This setting is achieved by the placement of light and dark sections of the blocks.

RED, GRAY, AND BLACK LOG CABIN

I was inspired by a printed fabric design that showed gray log cabin blocks with small amounts of red. I decided to make an improv log cabin quilt with gray, white, and black and just a little red in each block. I also used dark blue here and there. Then, just for fun (and to add interest), I used a blue center in one block and yellow in another, instead of the red used elsewhere. The result is a design with many interesting things to look at!

Vital Stats

Quilt size: 64″ x 80″ (162.6 x 203.2cm)
Block size: 8″ (20.3cm) square
Eighty blocks, ten rows of eight blocks

Tools and Materials

- Square ruler: 8½″ (21.6cm)
- Block centers and logs: Assorted scraps or fat quarters—both solids and prints—in gray, red, black, white, and dark blue (Yardage is not provided because of the use of scrap fabrics.)
- Accent fabric: Small amounts of yellow and blue fabrics
- Backing: 5 yards (457.2cm):
  Cut two 90″ (228.6cm) x WOF (42″ [106.7cm]) pieces
- Binding: ⅝ yards (57.1cm):
  Cut eight 2½″ (6.4cm) x WOF (42″ [106.7cm]) strips (or make scrappy binding)

Block Construction

This quilt has many variations between the blocks, but most of the blocks follow a regular improv log cabin format with a small red center. There are many variations in angles, color, value, and fabrics. Block Example 2 departs from the usual log cabin block construction, so details about how to make it are provided. Note: Only one triangle block in this quilt was made following the instructions in Example 2.

Block Example 1

1. Rough-cut a small red square or rectangle, 2″ to 3″ (5.1 to 7.6cm) for the starting center piece.

2. Add a round of logs of varying sizes, shapes, and colors around the center piece.

3. Keep adding logs in rounds until your block is at least 9″ (22.9cm) square. Trim your block to 8½″ (21.6cm) square.

IMPROVISATION TIPS

- Variations in fabric
- Different angles and width of logs
- Some repetition of pieced logs

Block Example 2

1. Cut a triangle with each side about 3″ (7.6cm)—even better if you can cut it from a pieced scrap. Start with one round of logs around the center triangle, then add several more rounds.

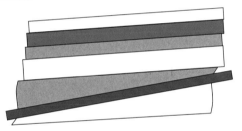

2. Make a string set, using the example shown as a guide. The partly made triangle section will be inserted into the pieced string set.

3. Place the triangle over the string set and cut on the left side (as shown by the orange lines). Sew the triangle to the string set. Then cut and sew the string set to the right side of the triangle. Sew both sides of the string set to the triangle and straighten the edges. Add logs to the top and bottom of the block to reach the size needed. Trim to 8½″ (21.6cm) square.

Make eighty blocks total.

Quilt Assembly

Arrange the blocks into ten rows of eight blocks, orienting them however you like. Sew the blocks in each row together using a ¼″ (6mm) seam. Press. Sew the rows together using a ¼″ (6mm) seam. Press.

Finishing the Quilt

1. The backing piece should be at least 72″ x 88″ (182.9 x 223.5cm). Sew two 88″ (223.5cm) x WOF (42″ [106.7cm]) strips together as shown after trimming off the selvages. Press the seam.

2. Layer the backing, batting, and quilt top together and baste. Quilt as desired.

3. Bind the quilt. See page 52 for binding instructions.

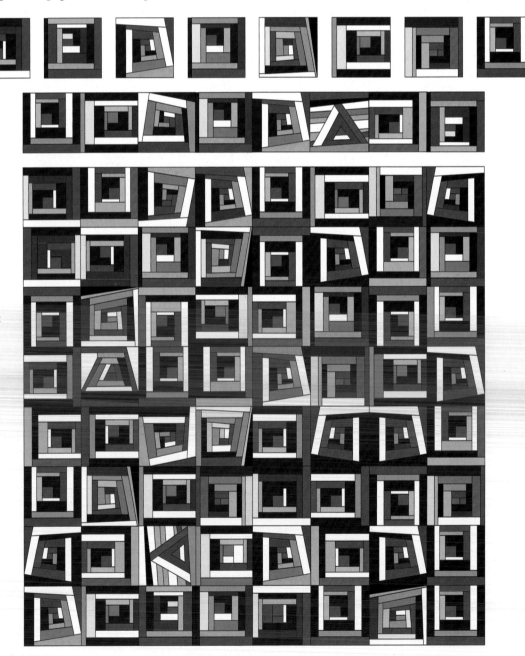

RED, WHITE, AND BLUE

This quilt was inspired by a group of blue fabrics and I decided that the quilt needed "something to look at" (otherwise known as a focal point). So I made blocks with red and a small number of larger blocks. I also used many geometric prints and curved joins within a number of the blocks. The controlled color palette of red, white, blue, black, and gray prints and solids helps unite this quilt.

Vital Stats

Quilt size: 62" x 78" (157.5 x 198.1cm)
Block sizes: 8" (20.3cm) square (sixteen red and thirty-eight blue blocks at this size)
12" (30.5cm) square (four blue blocks at this size)
First border: 1" (2.5cm) red fabric
Second border: 2" (5.1cm) black-on-white print

Quilted by **Yessant Habetz**

IMPROVISATION TIPS

- Skinny and narrow strips
- Angled/crooked logs
- Pieced logs
- Pieced centers
- Very small to medium centers

Tools and Materials

- Square rulers: 12½" (31.8cm) and 8½" (21.6cm)
- Blocks and logs: Assorted fabric scraps or fat quarters in red, blue, white, black, and gray, including geometric prints (Yardage is not provided because of the use of scrap fabrics.)
- First border: ⅜ yard (34.3cm) red fabric:
  Cut eight 1½" (3.8cm) x WOF (42" [106.7cm]) strips
- Second border: ½ yard (45.7cm) black-on-white print fabric:
  Cut eight 2½" (6.4cm) x WOF (42" [106.7cm]) strips
- Backing: 5 yards (457.2cm):
  Cut two 86" (218.4cm) x WOF (42" [106.7cm]) pieces
- Binding: ½ yard (45.7cm):
  Cut eight 2½" (6.4cm) x WOF (42" [106.7cm]) (or make scrappy binding)

Block Construction

The following instructions are general because of the varied nature of these blocks. Refer to the basic log cabin instructions (page 11) and the techniques in Chapter 2 as needed for more information on specific techniques. For example, I used curved joins quite often when making the blocks, as you can see in the project photos.

Blue Blocks

1. Start the blocks with a small to medium center, 1" to 3" (2.5 to 7.6cm), made of either a single fabric or small pieces of fabric sewn together. The illustration shows a small center with a couple of logs added.

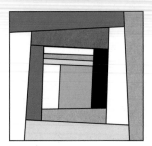

2. Before adding a log, trim the edge straight. Or, if doing a curved join, cut both the block-in-progress and the new log with the same gentle curve.

3. Press away from the center after adding each log. Vary the fabrics used for the logs and include angled logs, skinny strips, selvage logs, and pieced logs as desired.

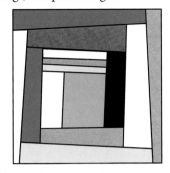

4. When the block is large enough, trim to size.

Make thirty-eight 8½″ (21.6cm) blue blocks.
Make four 12½″ (31.8cm) blue blocks.

Red Blocks

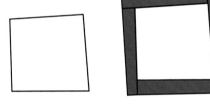

1. Make a square-like center piece, 2½″ to 3″ (6.4 to 7.6cm), from black-on-white print fabric. Use fairly narrow red logs for the first round around the center.

2. For subsequent rounds of logs, use any of the red, gray, black, and white prints. Before adding new logs, trim the edge straight. Or, if doing a curved join, cut both the block-in-progress and the new log with the same gentle curve. Press away from the center after adding each log.

3. Vary the fabrics used and include angled logs, skinny strips, selvage logs, and pieced logs as desired.

4. When the block is large enough, trim to size.

Make sixteen 8½″ (21.6cm) red blocks.

Quilt Assembly

Quilt Center
Refer to project layout diagram when sewing blocks together. Sew all blocks together using a ¼″ (6mm) seam. Press the seams.

1. Sew two rows of seven 8½″ (21.6cm) blue blocks together for the top of the quilt and sew two rows of seven 8½″ (21.6cm) blue blocks together for the bottom of the quilt.

2. Sew the four 12½″ (31.8cm) blue blocks together for the center of the quilt.

3. Sew two three-block columns of 8½″ (21.6cm) red blocks.

4. Sew two rows of five 8½″ (21.6cm) red blocks.

5. Sew two columns of five 8½″ (21.6cm) blue blocks. At this point, all the pieces are ready to be put together from top to bottom following the project layout diagram.

Border Assembly

First Border
1. Remove any selvages and sew the 1½″ (3.8cm) border strips into one long strip.

2. Measure the quilt from side to side. Cut two border sections to this length. Sew the top and bottom borders in place with a ¼″ (6mm) seam. Press away from the center.

3. Measure the length of the quilt with the top and bottom borders on. Cut two border pieces to this length. Sew the right and left borders in place with a ¼″ (6mm) seam. Press away from the center.

Second Border
1. Remove the selvages and sew the 2½″ (6.4cm) border strips into one long strip.

2. Measure the quilt from side to side. Cut two border sections to this length. Sew the top and bottom borders in place with a ¼″ (6mm) seam. Press away from the center.

3. Measure the length of the quilt with the top and bottom borders on. Cut two border pieces to this length. Sew the right and left borders in place with a ¼″ (6mm) seam. Press away from the center.

Finishing the Quilt

1. The backing piece should be at least 70″ x 86″ (177.8 x 218.4cm). Sew two 86″ (218.4cm) x WOF (42″ [106.7cm]) strips together as shown after trimming off the selvages. Press the seam.

2. Layer the backing, batting, and quilt top together and baste. Quilt as desired.

3. Bind the quilt. See page 52 for binding instructions.

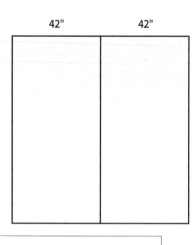

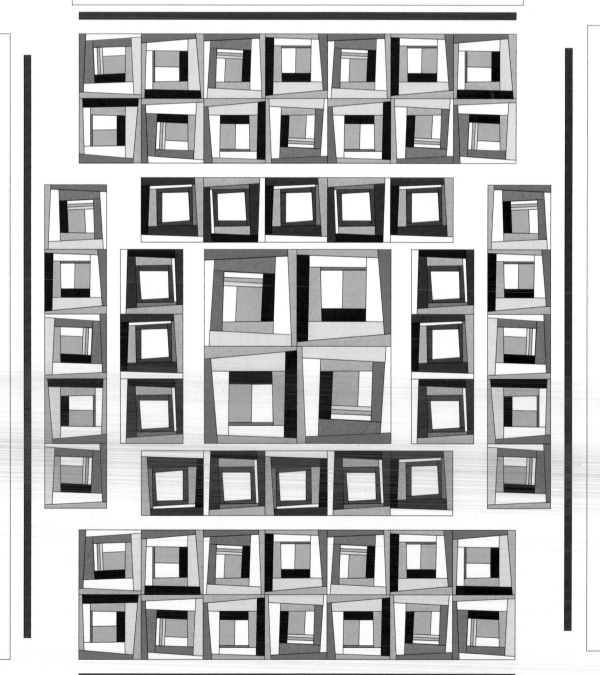

FLOATING LOG CABINS

In the Floating Log Cabins quilt, the irregularly shaped colored sections seem to dance on the background. Easy to make with some leftover prints and solids, this quilt has a really fun vibe and went together quickly. I used the same fabric for the center of each block, but using different fabrics would also work. I also added a scrappy border. I quilted this by hand with big stitch quilting.

Vital Stats

Quilt size: 36½" x 47" (92.7 x 119.4cm)
Block size: 10½" (27.7cm) square
Twelve blocks, four rows of three blocks

IMPROVISATION TIPS

- Angled or crooked logs
- Narrow or skinny string inserts or joins
- Curved skinny inserts
- Selvage logs

Tools and Materials

- Cutting mat large enough to square up blocks
- Block centers: One fat quarter or enough scrap fabric to make twelve 3" to 5" (7.6 to 12.7cm) rough-cut squares
- Blocks: Assorted prints (Yardage is not provided because of the use of scrap fabrics.)
- Background: 3 to 4 yards (274.3 to 365.8cm) white (or other color) fabric
- Backing: 2⅝ yards (240cm):
  Cut two 45" (114.3cm) x WOF (42" [106.7cm]) pieces
- Borders: ⅜ yard (34.3cm):
  Cut four 3" (7.6cm) x WOF (42" [106.7cm]) pieces or use mixed 3" (7.6cm) strips
- Binding: ⅜ yard (34.3cm) white fabric:
  Cut five 2½" (6.4cm) x WOF (42" [106.7cm]) strips (or make a scrappy binding)

Block Construction

1. Start with a 3″ to 5″ (7.6 to 12.7cm) rough-cut square. Add logs around the center in rounds (see page 51 for Block Construction in Beginner's Log Cabin Improv for specific details) until the cabin block is about 6″ to 8″ (15.2 to 20.3cm) in length and width (it does not have to be square at this point). Make twelve blocks this way, varying the size, shape, and orientation of these sections to add interest to the quilt.

2. Add background pieces to make the blocks into square log cabin blocks, making sure that the blocks are big enough to trim to 11″ (27.9cm).

TIP

Cutting the background pieces so that the outside edges are on the grain (instead of on the bias) will make the blocks more stable and easier to put together.

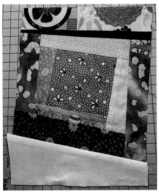

2a. One piece of background fabric is already sewn into place.

2b. An oversized piece of background fabric is ready for cutting. Place the background fabric under the block in progress.

2c. The background fabric is right side up and aligned vertically on the ruler line. The block-in-progress is ready for cutting on the angle identified by the line so that the angles match. Cut with a ruler and rotary cutter.

2d. The cut background piece has the same angle as the edge of the log cabin with the rightmost edge on the straight of the grain.

2e. The background fabric is sewn into place, pressed, and rotated.

2f. The block has the background fabric tucked underneath and the right side up, ready for cutting.

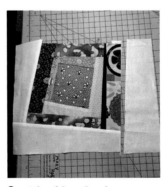

2g. The fabric has been cut so that the angles match and the right outside edge will be on the straight of grain.

2h. The right side of the background fabric is face down and ready to sew in place. Add background fabric in the same way to the fourth side.

3. Trim the block to 11″ (27.9cm) square.

Make twelve blocks.

Quilt Assembly

1. Arrange the blocks into four rows of three blocks (see project layout). Sew the blocks in each row together using a ¼″ (6mm) seam. Press. Sew the rows together using a ¼″ (6mm) seam. Press.

2. Sew the 3″ (7.6cm) border pieces together to make one long piece.

3. Starting at one corner, add the long border strip along one side. Trim, then continue adding the border to the adjacent side. Trim and continue in this way until the border has been sewn around the entire quilt center.

Finishing the Quilt

1. The backing piece should be at least 44½″ x 55″ (113 x 139.7cm). Sew two 45″ (114.3cm) x WOF (42″ [106.7cm]) pieces together as shown after trimming off selvages. Press the seam.

2. Layer the backing, batting, and quilt top together and baste. Quilt as desired.

3. Bind the quilt. See page 52 for binding instructions.

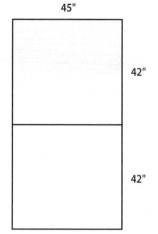

WONKY LOG CABIN WITH LINES

High-contrast skinny-string joins reveal the structure in this quilt. Most blocks have three rounds of logs joined around the center piece, and you can use this technique with regular or crooked logs. This quilt has both regular and crooked logs.

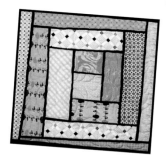   

Vital Stats

Quilt size: 60″ x 84″ (152.4 x 213.4cm)
Block size: 12″ (30.5cm) square
Sashing: ¼″ (6mm)
Thirty-five blocks, seven rows of five blocks

Tools and Materials

- 12½″ (31.8cm) square ruler
- Block centers: ½ yard (45.7cm):
  Cut when making the blocks
- Logs: Thirty-five fat quarters or equivalent scraps (about one fat quarter per block):
  Cut when making the blocks
- Skinny joins and skinny sashing: 3 yards (274.3cm):
  Cut ¾″ (1.9cm) x WOF (42″ [106.7 cm]) strips
  Note: Cut ten to twenty ¾″ (1.9cm) strips as you need them, instead of cutting all the strips at once
- Backing: 5⅛ yards (468.6cm):
  Cut two 92″ (233.7cm) x WOF (42″ [106.7 cm]) pieces
- Binding: ⅝ yard (57.2cm) of the same fabric used for the skinny string joins:
  Cut eight 2½″ (6.4cm) x WOF (42″ [106.7 cm]) strips

TIP

For consistent ¼″ (6mm) skinny string joins, follow this advice: Make sure you can see the previous seam. Sew ¼″ (6mm) from the *previous seam*. The photo shows how I use my foot and needle to get a consistent distance between the seams.

Block Construction

Most logs should be approximately 2″ to 2½″ (5.1 to 6.4cm) wide, but I like to add extra-wide logs on the third round to make finishing and trimming these blocks easier.

1. Cut a fabric piece about 3″ (7.6cm) square for the block center. Have some ¾″ (1.9cm) skinny contrast strips ready to go.

1a. Cut a rectangle longer than needed and about 2″ to 2½″ (5.1 to 6.4cm) wide (this is piece 1A).

1b. Sew a skinny strip to one side of the 1A piece with a ¼″ (6mm) seam and press the seam away from the skinny strip (see page 39). Now you have a 1A log plus skinny strip.

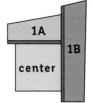

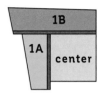

1c. Sew the skinny strip side of the 1A log plus skinny strip to the righthand side of the center with a ¼″ (6mm) seam.

1d. Press both seams away from the center, rotate 90 degrees to the left, trim the edge, and prepare to add the next piece.

2. Cut a rectangle longer than needed and about 2″ to 2½″ (5.1 to 6.4cm) wide (this is piece 1B).

2a. Sew a skinny strip to one side of the 1B piece and press the seam away from the skinny strip.

2b. Sew the skinny strip side of the 1B plus skinny strip to the righthand side of the center.

2c. Press both seams away from the center, rotate 90 degrees to the left, trim the edge, and prepare to add the next piece.

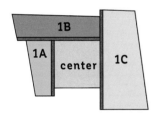

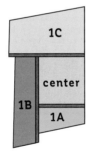

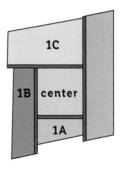

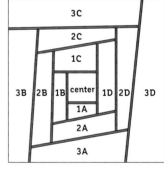

3. Select and cut a new rectangle about 2″ to 2½″ (5.1 to 6.4cm) wide (this is piece 1C), add a skinny strip to 1C, press, and then add the 1C piece plus skinny strip to the righthand side of the center.

3a. Rotate 90 degrees to the left and trim the edge.

3b. Continue in this manner to complete the second round.

3c. Complete the third round with extra-wide logs to make the blocks easier to trim to size.

> **TIP**
>
> When cutting the skinny strips for joins and sashing, cut ten to twenty strips at a time to reduce wrinkling and tangling. (Refer back to page 39 for more on skinny string joins.)

Quilt Assembly

1. Arrange the blocks into seven rows of five blocks. Cut twenty-eight ¾″ (1.9cm) strips the length of the blocks for sashing. Sew the strips between blocks in each row as each row is sewn.

2. Measure the width of the rows and prepare four ¾″ (1.9cm) strips of that length. Sew one strip of fabric between each row as the rows are sewn to each other.

3. Do not add a strip to the top and bottom or to the sides of the quilt.

Finishing the Quilt

1. The backing piece should be at least 68″ (173cm) x 92″ (234cm). Sew the two 92″ (234cm) x WOF (42″ [106.7cm]) pieces together as shown after trimming off the selvages. Press seam.

2. Layer the backing, batting and quilt top together and baste. Quilt as desired.

3. Bind the quilt. See page 52 for binding instructions.

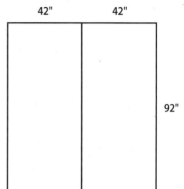

Wonky Log Cabin with Lines **81**

SELVAGE LOG CABIN

I enjoy adding a selvage piece here and there in my log cabins and string quilts. I decided to go all the way with this one, so even the binding and backing are made from selvages. This quilt has many differently shaped block centers and many different types of selvages. In one block, I used yellow selvages from the same fabric, and the dark block uses only selvages without a light edge. Writing or illustrations on the selvages and the bit of white in these strips provide the eye with something different.

Vital Stats

Quilt size: 52″ x 64″ (132.1 x 162.6 cm)
Block size: 12″ (30.5cm) square
Border: 2″ (5.1cm)
Twenty blocks, five rows of four blocks

Quilted by **Yessant Habetz**

WORKING WITH SELVAGES

- Save selvages in a big bag or a bin.
- When cutting off selvages, include some fabric print with the white and keep the strips at least 1½″ (3.8cm) wide.
- Save selvages from lengths of backing fabric.
- Sew selvage logs right side up with a zigzag stitch.

Tools and Materials

- 12½″ (31.8cm) square ruler
- Block centers: ½ yard (45.7cm) fabric for block centers:
  Cut when making the blocks
- Selvage logs: Use your collection of selvage strips or make a block at a time as you collect selvages (Yardage is not provided because there is no yardage equivalent for selvages.):
  Cut to size as you make the blocks
- Border: ½ yard (45.7cm):
  Cut seven 2½″ (6.4cm) x WOF (42″ [106.7cm]) strips
- Backing: 3½ yards (320cm):
  Cut two 60″ (152.4cm) x WOF (42″ [106.7cm]) pieces
- Binding: Make one long 240″ (610cm) binding strip by sewing 1½″ (3.8cm) selvages together end to end on the diagonal or cut seven 2½″ (6.4cm) x WOF (42″ [106.7cm]) strips. (I used mostly long length selvages cut from backing fabric leftovers.)

Block Construction

1. Cut a center shape. While these diagrams show a five-sided center, these instructions work for any three- to six-sided shape. Select a log with a selvage edge. Place the selvage edge right side up, covering the edge of the center piece by ⅜″ (1cm). Sew the selvage log into place with a zigzag stitch. Press.

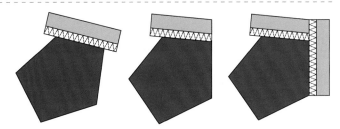

2. Turn the block to the left so that there is an edge to trim and sew. Trim the edge straight. Select a selvage log, overlap it by ⅜″ (1cm), and sew it into place. Press.

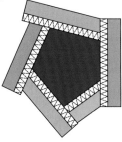

3. Continue turning, trimming, adding new selvage logs, and pressing until all edges of the block center are surrounded. (**Note**: The last selvage log in the first round overlaps the first selvage log.)

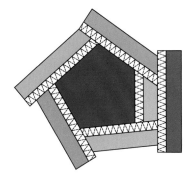

4. Start adding the second round of selvage logs.

5. Continue adding rounds of selvage logs. When the block is large enough, add selvage logs to fill out the corners as shown in this photo. Continue until the block is large enough to trim to 12½″ (31.8cm).

Make twenty blocks.

JOINING SELVAGE LOGS

Place the selvage edge right side up on the raw edge of the log cabin, overlapping by at least ⅜″ (1cm). Pin it into place and use a zigzag or utility zigzag stitch to sew the selvage edge to the fabric underneath. If you use a straight stitch, sew very close to the selvage edge. My favorite stitch to use is the utility, or three step, zigzag shown in the diagram. Test the zigzag for desired stitch length and width.

IMPROVISATION TIPS

1. Use selvage logs with different colors and values.

2. Use crooked selvage logs and logs from the source fabric in different widths.

3. Select sections of selvages that have interesting writing, colored dots, or pictures.

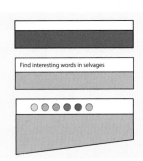

Find interesting words in selvages

Quilt Assembly
Quilt Center

Arrange blocks into five rows of four blocks. Sew the blocks in each row together using a ¼″ (6mm) seam. Press. Sew the rows together using a ¼″ (6mm) seam. Press.

Border

1. Remove selvages and sew the 2½″ (6.4cm) border strips into one long strip.

2. Measure the quilt from side to side. Cut two border sections to this length. Sew the top and bottom borders in place with a ¼″ (6mm) seam. Press away from the center.

3. Measure the length of the quilt with the top and bottom borders on. Cut two border pieces to this length. Sew the right and left borders in place with a ¼″ (6mm) seam. Press away from the center.

Finishing the Quilt

1. The backing piece should be at least 60″ x 72″ (152.4 x 182.9cm). Sew the two 60″ (152.4cm) x WOF (42″ [106.7cm]) pieces together as shown after trimming off the selvages. Press the seam.

2. Layer the backing, batting, and quilt top together and baste. Quilt as desired.

3. If using yardage instead of selvage binding, apply binding as described on page 52 or bind the quilt using the pieced 240″ x 1½″ (610 x 3.8cm) selvages. This is a single fold binding. Sew the *raw edge* of the binding strip right sides together to the edge of the quilt back. Fold at the corners in the same way as is done for regular binding (page 52). After attaching the binding strip, fold around the edges and topstitch with a straight or zigzag stitch to the front side of the quilt.

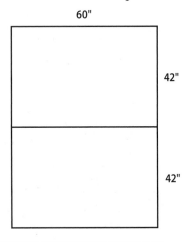

60″

42″

42″

Front corner of quilt. The binding is mitered at the corner and sewn on the front with a straight stitch.

The binding shown from the quilt back at the corner.

Quilt back

MIXED MEDIA

Inspired by seeing cigar-ribbon quilts, I started saving the ties from precut fabric bundles from fabric manufacturers and quilt stores. For this project, I also gathered trims, printed and plain ribbons, zippers, and narrow, flat cotton lace, all of which are not typically used in quilts. For this quilt, I used my collection of these materials on solid and solid-like fabric logs along with angled logs and a single prairie point as my improv elements. See Chapter 2 for more details on adding these materials to your quilt.

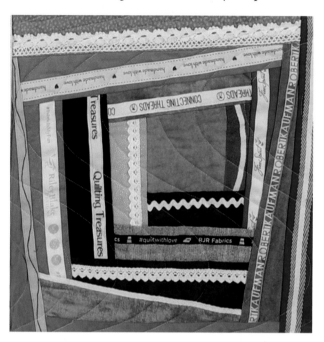

Vital Stats

Quilt size: 58″ x 72½″ (147.3 x 184.2cm)
Block size: 14½″ (36.8cm) square
Twenty blocks, five rows of four blocks

Quilted by **Yessant Habetz**

IMPROVISATION TIPS

- Angled logs
- Varying color and value
- Adding a zipper
- Skip the prints on this project. There is already a lot going on with trims.

Tools and Materials

- Cutting mat large enough to trim 15″ (38.1cm) blocks
- Blocks: Assorted solid and solid-like blender fabrics, scraps, or fat quarters (Yardage is not provided because of the use of scrap fabrics.)
- Assorted embellishments: Ribbons, twill tape (plain and decorative), lace, rickrack, and zippers
- Backing: 3¾ yards (342.9cm):
  Cut two 66″ (167.6cm) x WOF (42″ [106.7cm]) pieces
- Binding: ⅝ yard (57.2cm):
  Cut eight 2½″ (6.4cm) x WOF (42″ [106.7cm]) strips (or make scrappy binding)

Block Construction

Most of these blocks have a 5″ to 6″ (12.7 to 15.2cm) centers and three rounds of logs that are 2½″ to 3″ (6.4 to 7.6cm) wide before joining.

1. Cut a 5″ to 6″ (12.7 to 15.2cm) square-like piece for the block center.

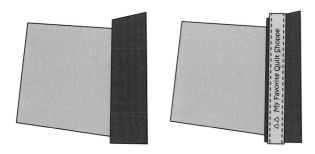

2. Join a log to one side of the center. If desired, add embellishments to each log before adding the next log. (**Note**: I usually place the ribbon or other embellishment close to the join, but with some of the fabric showing, and sew a straight stitch on both sides of the new addition. The dashed lines indicate stitching lines. For any directional embellishment, I always consider the center of the block as up.)

3. Rotate the block to the left, trim the edge, and join another log. Press. Add embellishments and press.

4. Continue adding logs in the same way until the block is large enough. Rotate the block to the left, trim the edge, and join another log. Press and add embellishments. Trim to 15″ (38.1cm).

Make twenty blocks.

HOW DIFFERENT CAN A BLOCK BE?

This block was made to demonstrate the use of unusual materials. This block uses only black, purples, and white, with a few white embellishments. This has a more sophisticated and calmer look compared to the Mixed Media quilt which uses loads of colors and an embellishment on nearly every log.

Quilt Assembly

Arrange the blocks into five rows of four blocks. Sew the blocks in each row together using a ¼″ (6mm) seam. Press. Sew the rows together using a ¼″ (6mm) seam. Press.

Finishing the Quilt

1. The backing piece should be at least 66″ x 80.5″ (167.6 x 204.5cm). Sew two 66″ (167.6cm) x WOF (42″ [106.7cm]) pieces together as shown after trimming off the selvages. Press the seam.

2. Layer the backing, batting, and quilt top together and baste. Quilt as desired.

3. Bind the quilt. See page 52 for binding instructions.

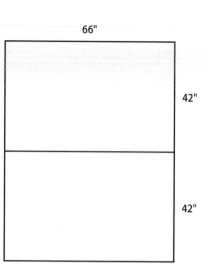

HALF LOG CABIN VARIATION

Half log cabin blocks start in a corner, with logs added to two sides, instead of four sides, of the starting piece, hence the name. See also pages 11 and 33 for more details on the half log cabin block.

This is a more orderly improvisational piece than most of the others in this book. I started with leftover fabric from a project I had decided not to complete. I had seven different colors with five or six fabrics in each color. I had already cut multiple 1½" (3.8cm) strips from fat quarters, and I had some uncut fabric from which I made some 2" (5.1cm) strips. I decided to throw in skinny white joins as well.

The improvisational part was to vary the placement of colors and log sizes between sets of blocks. Each block requires a 4½" (11.4cm) square starting piece, three sets of 1½" (3.8cm) strips, two sets of 2" (5.1cm) strips, and one ¾" (1.9cm) skinny strip. I made sets of four blocks that were the same in terms of color, color location, and strip size, but with different fabrics.

Vital Stats

Quilt size: 57" x 76" (144.8 x 193cm)
Block size: 9½" (24.1cm)
Forty-eight blocks, eight rows of six blocks

Quilted by **Yessant Habetz**

Tools and Materials

- Block centers and logs: Assorted fabrics in six to seven color groupings. Leftover chunks of fabric are useful for this project, while very small scraps are not. (Yardage is not provided because of the use of scrap fabrics.)
  Block centers: 4½" (11.4cm) squares
  Logs: Cut 2" (5.1 cm) and 1½" (3.8 cm) colored strips and ¾" (1.9cm) white fabric strips
- Backing: At least 3¾ yards (342.9cm):
  Cut two 65" (165.1cm) x WOF (42" [106.7 cm]) pieces
- Binding: ⅝ yard (57.2cm):
  Cut eight 2½" (6.4cm) x WOF (42" [106.7 cm]) strips

Block Construction

Work in sets of four blocks, keeping the location of the colors and the width of the strips the same in each set of four blocks. Each set of blocks should use three rounds of 1½" (3.8cm) strips, two rounds of 2" (5.1cm) strips, and one round of ¾" (1.9cm) skinny strings. See 39 for more details on skinny stings in joins. (**Note**: I placed the skinny string neither right next to the center nor at the outer edges of the blocks.)

1. Use a 4½" (11.4cm) center. Select two strips of the same hue, but different fabrics.

2. Sew a strip to one side, using a ¼" (6mm) seam allowance. Press away from the center.

3. Rotate left and trim the right edge.

4. Add the other strip of the same hue to the adjoining side. Press away from the center.

5. Select two strips of the same hue but different fabrics. Rotate the block to the right. Trim the right edge.

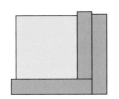

6. Sew a strip to one side. Press away from the center after adding each strip.

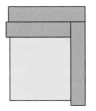

7. Rotate left and trim the right edge.

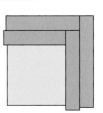

8. Add the other strip of the same hue to the adjoining side. Press away from the center.

9. Continue to add strips to adjacent sides, trimming the edges before adding the next strip. Press away from the center.

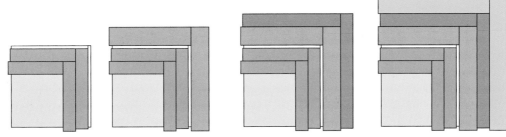

Each set of blocks should use three rounds of 1½" (3.8cm) strips, two rounds of 2" (5.1cm) strips, and one round of ¾" (1.9cm) skinny strings.

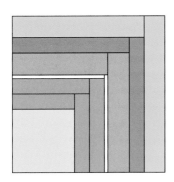

10. Trim each block to 10" (25.4cm) using a square ruler or cutting mat.

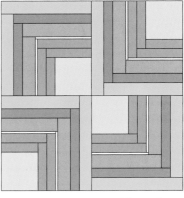

11. Put the blocks together in sets of four. Shown is one example, but you may put them together any way you like.

Quilt Assembly

Arrange the sets of four blocks into four rows of three. Sew the sets of four blocks in each row together using a ¼" (6mm) seam. Press. Sew the rows together using a ¼" (6mm) seam. Press.

Finishing the Quilt

1. The backing piece should be at least 65" x 84" (165.1 x 213.4cm). Sew two 65" (165.1cm) x WOF (42" [106.7cm]) strips together as shown after trimming off the selvages. Press the seam open.

2. Layer the backing, batting, and quilt top together and baste. Quilt as desired.

3. Bind the quilt. See page 52 for binding instructions.

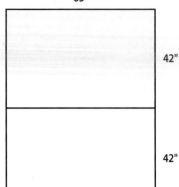

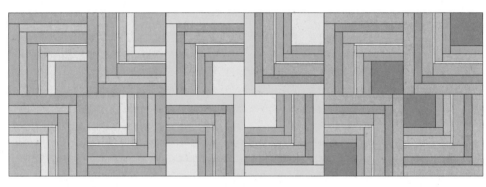

COURTHOUSE STEPS

Courthouse steps blocks are made by sewing logs to opposite sides of the center and then adding logs to the other two sides. From the many possible layouts, I chose to use very light fabrics alternating with dark fabrics and square red centers.

Vital Stats

Quilt size: 70″ x 80″ (177.8 x 203.2cm)
Block size: 10″ (25.4cm)
Fifty-six blocks, eight rows of seven blocks

Quilted by **Yessant Habetz**

IMPROVISATION TIPS

- Skinny strings
- Logs made from two narrow pieces
- Logs of varying widths
- Angled logs

Tools and Materials

- 10½″ (26.7cm) square ruler
- Block centers: ½ yard (45.7cm) red fabric:
    Cut five 3½″ (8.9cm) x WOF (42″ [106.7cm]) strips:
        Subcut fifty-six 3½″ (8.9cm) squares (each strip yields twelve squares)
- Logs: Dark and light fabrics (Yardage is not provided because of the use of scrap fabrics.)
    Cut 1¾″ (4.4cm), 2″ (5.1cm), and 2½″ (6.4cm) strips
- Backing: 5 yards (457.2cm):
    Cut into two 2½-yard (229cm) pieces
- Binding: ⅝ yard (57.2cm) red fabric:
    Cut nine 2½″ (6.4cm) x WOF (42″ [106.7cm]) strips

Block Construction

1. Use a 3½″ (8.9cm) center square.

2. Sew a light log to the right and left side of the center square, using a ¼″ (6mm) seam. Open and press. (**Note:** While the diagrams show straight rectangles and cuts, I made slight angles when cutting to add interest.)

3. Rotate and trim edges before adding new logs.

4. Sew a dark log to the right and left side of the center square, using a ¼″ (6mm) seam. Open and press.

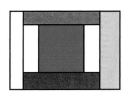
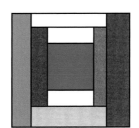
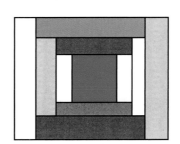
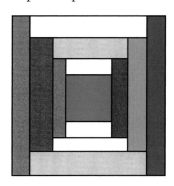

5. Continue to add logs to opposite sides using the same process. Trim the edges, add the light or dark logs, open and press. Alternate between light and dark. For nearly all the blocks, three logs were added on each side. Add more logs as needed to reach the correct size.

6. Trim blocks to 10½″ (26.7cm).

Make fifty-six blocks.

TIP

Plan ahead as you add logs so that your blocks will be large enough to trim to 10½" (26.7cm) square.

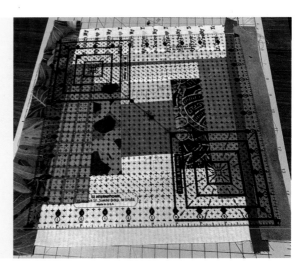

Quilt Assembly

Arrange the blocks into seven columns of eight blocks. Sew the blocks in each column together using a ¼″ (6mm) seam. Press. Sew the columns together using a ¼″ (6mm) seam. Press.

Finishing the Quilt

1. The backing piece should be at least 78″ x 88″ (198.1 x 223.5cm). Sew two 90″ (228.6cm) x WOF (42″ [106.7cm]) strips together as shown after trimming off the selvages. Press the seam open.

2. Layer the backing, batting, and quilt top together and baste. Quilt as desired.

3. Bind the quilt. See page 52 for binding instructions.

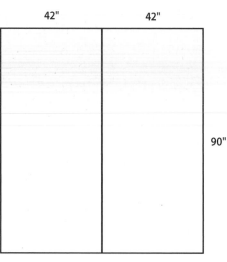

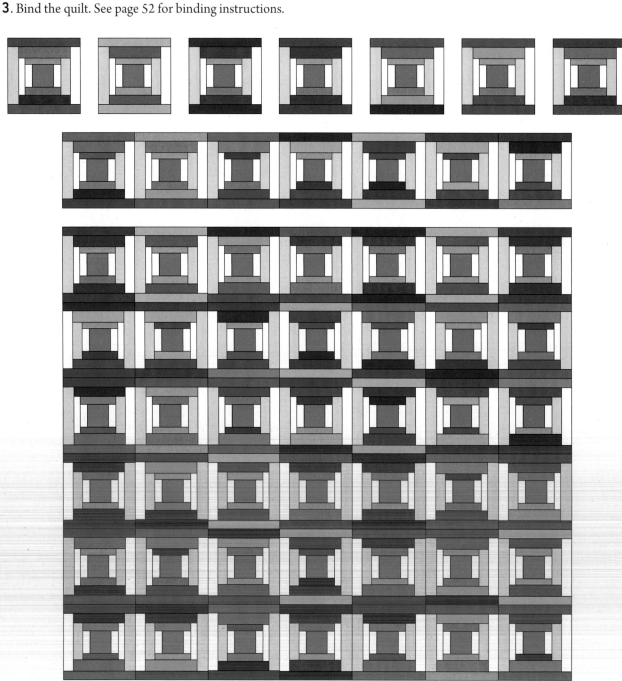

BLACK WONKY PINEAPPLE

To me, these slightly wonky pineapple blocks seem to dance against the black background. This project uses 2½″ (6.4cm) strips of fabric for the pineapple blocks. Each block uses five different fabrics of the same color: one for the center piece, and the other four for each round of the block. An exception is the block in the lower right in the project photo, which was made with a fat quarter of ombre fabric. Black background fabric provides great contrast with the colored blocks. Another option is to use any blue fabric in the blue block or any pink fabric in the pink block, rather than using the same fabric in each round.

Vital Stats

Quilt size: 66″ x 82½″ (167.6 x 209.6cm)
Block size: 16½″ (41.9cm) square
Twenty blocks, five rows of four blocks

Quilted by **Yessant Habetz**

IMPROVISATION TIPS

There is already plenty of improv with the angled cuts, so don't add much more. For example, you could consider adding an accent color in several blocks.

Tools and Materials

- Black background fabric: 6½ yards (594.4cm):
  1) Cut eight 8″ (20.3cm) x WOF (42″ [106.7cm]):
     Subcut forty 8″ (20.3cm) squares (each strip yields five squares) and cut each square diagonally into two half-square triangles (HSTs) (each pineapple block requires four HSTs to finish the corners)
  2) Cut sixty 2½″ (6.4cm) x WOF (42″ [106.7cm]) strips for blocks
- Colored fabric for blocks: Assorted scrap fabrics: one color per pineapple block (the equivalent of about one fat quarter total for each block):
  Cut one 4″ (10.2cm) square for each block center and 2½″ (6.4cm) strips of fabric as needed
- Backing: 5¼ yards (480.1cm):
  Cut two 90½″ (229.9cm) x WOF (42″ [106.7cm]) pieces
- Binding: ¾ yard (68.6cm):
  Cut nine 2½″ (6.4cm) x WOF (42″ [106.7cm]) strips (or make scrappy binding)

Block Construction

Note: Make the first part of the block carefully; the wonkiness comes a bit later. Use a ¼" (6mm) seam allowance throughout. Press away from the center after adding each piece of fabric.

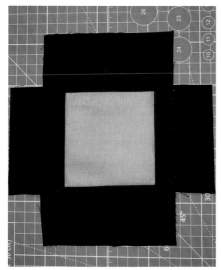

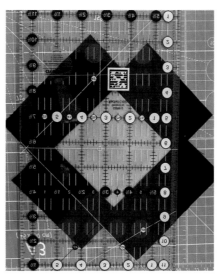

1. Start with a 4" (10.2cm) square of fabric. Sew two 4" x 2½" (10.2 x 6.4cm) strips to opposite sides. Sew two 5" x 2½" (12.7 x 6.4cm) strips to the other two sides.

2. Trim the block. Place the ruler so that a straight line passes through the center square from corner to corner and the ruler is ¼" (6mm) beyond the corner. Cut off the excess fabric to the right of the ruler.

3.Trim each of the corners in the same way. The trimmed block is shown here.

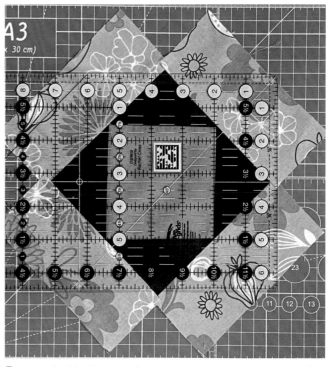

4. Add 2½" (6.4cm) strips of fabric the same length as the block to opposite sides of the block. Add 2 ½" (6.4cm) strips of fabric to the other two sides so that they overlap the previous two strips by at least ½" (1.3cm).

5. Trim the block using the same instructions as Step 2 and 3.

6. The trimmed block is ready for the next round of black strips.

7. Add the next set of 2½″ (6.4cm) black strips. They should be long enough to almost cover the sides of the green strips as shown in this photograph.

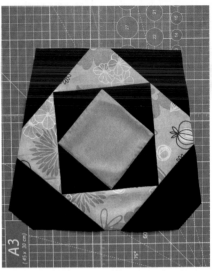

8. Now it's time to start developing the wonky parts of this block. In a regular pineapple block, this cut would be perpendicular to a straight line passing through the center square from corner to corner. Instead, trim the block using slight angles. **Note:** the center square is now tilted.

9. Add the next set of 2½″ (6.4cm) color strips. They should be long enough to almost cover the sides of the previous black strips as shown. Trim all four sides at a slight angle.

10. Add 2½″ (6.4cm) black strips. They should be long enough to almost cover each side of the block. Trim the black pieces at a slight angle. These photos show the block before (left) and after (right) trimming.

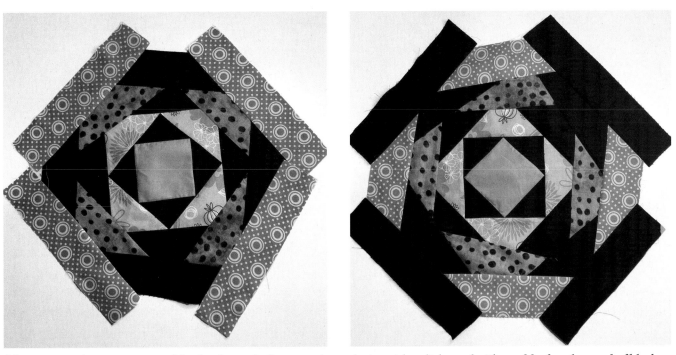

11. Continue the same way to add a third round of green strips and trim with a slight angle. Then add a fourth round of black strips and trim, again with a slight angle.

12. Add the fourth round of green strips and trim at a slight angle.

13. To finish the block use the large black HSTs cut from 8″ (20.3cm) squares. Arrange four of the triangles as shown. Sew the HSTs on the corners of the block with a ¼″ (6mm) seam.

14. Check the size of your blocks and trim to match the smallest block. I trimmed my blocks to 17″ (43.2cm) square. Occasionally, I had to add an extra black piece to make the block large enough. (This is because cutting at an angle leads to irregular sizes.)

Make twenty blocks, using a different color in each block.

Quilt Assembly

Arrange the blocks into five rows of four blocks. Sew the blocks in each row together using a ¼″ (6mm) seam. Press. Sew the rows together using a ¼″ (6mm) seam. Press.

Finishing the Quilt

1. The backing piece should be at least 74″ x 90½″ (188 x 229.9cm). Sew two 90½″ (229.9cm) strips together as shown after removing the selvages. Press the seam.

2. Layer the backing, batting, and quilt top together and baste. Quilt as desired.

3. Bind the quilt. See page 52 for binding instructions.

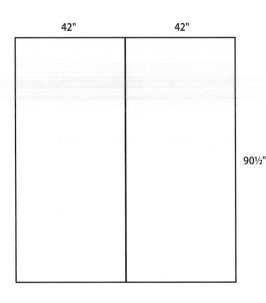

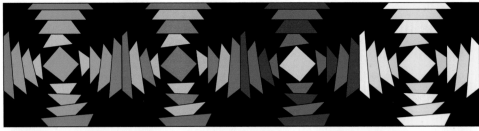

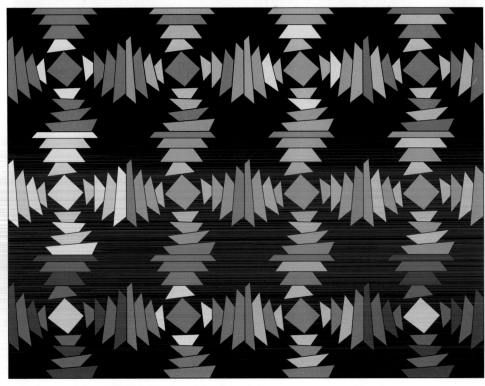

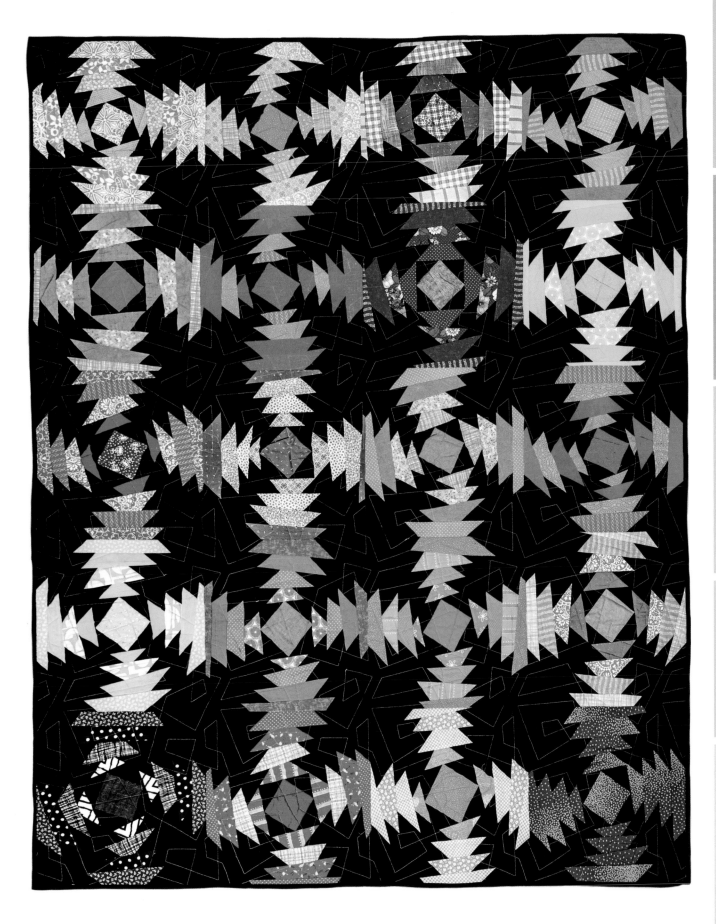

WHITE WONKY PINEAPPLE

This wonky pineapple quilt is a great way to show off fabric scraps. Cut scraps into 2″ (5.1cm) strips. Alternate rounds of white and print scraps and use the wonky pineapple technique to make these amusing pineapple blocks. I made four blocks using pink background fabric.

Vital Stats

Quilt size: 66″ x 76″ (167.6 x 193cm)
Block size: 10″ (25.4 cm) square
Border: 3″ (7.6cm)
Forty-two blocks, seven rows of six blocks

Quilted by **Yessant Habetz**

IMPROVISATION TIPS

I don't recommend doing any other improv in these blocks besides changing the fabric and playing with angles.

Tools and Materials

- 10½″ (26.7cm) square ruler
- White background fabric: 9 yards (823cm):
  1) Cut twelve 6″ (15.2cm) x WOF (42″ [106.7cm]) strips: Subcut eighty-four 6″ (15.2cm) squares (each strip yields seven squares), then cut each square diagonally into two HSTs (each pineapple block requires four HSTs to finish the corners).
  2) Cut eighty-four 2″ (5.1cm) x WOF (42″ [106.7cm]) strips (each block requires two or three of these strips). I cut these in small batches as I worked on the quilt. Cut additional strips if needed.
- Pink background fabric: 1 yard (91.4cm)
  Cut 2″ (5.1cm) strips of fabric as needed
- Print fabrics for blocks: Assorted scrap fabrics (Yardage is not provided because of the use of scrap fabrics.)
  Cut one 2½″ (6.4cm) square for each block center and 2″ (5.1cm) strips of fabric as needed.
- Backing: 4⅜ yards (400.1cm):
  Cut two 74″ (188cm) x WOF (42″ [106.7cm]) pieces.
- Border: 1 yard (91.4cm):
  Cut eight 3½″ (8.9cm) x WOF (42″ [106.7cm]) strips.
- Binding: ⅝ yard (57.2cm):
  Cut eight 2½″ (6.4cm) x WOF (42″ [106.7cm]) strips (or make scrappy binding, as I did in the quilt shown).

Block Construction

Make the first part of the block carefully; the wonkiness comes a bit later. Press well away from the center after adding each piece of fabric. **Note:** Use these simplified instructions for wonky pineapple blocks. If needed, refer to the more detailed photos found in the instructions for the Black Wonky Pineapple, page 98. Keep in mind that this quilt uses 2½" (6.4cm) centers and 2" (5.1cm) wide strips.

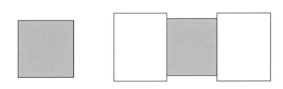

1. Use a 2½" (6.4cm) square of fabric for the center. Using a ¼" (6mm) seam, sew 2" (5.1cm) strips of white background fabric to opposite sides of the center. These strips should be at least 2½" (6.4cm) long. Press the seams away from the center.

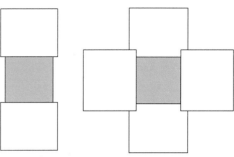

2. Turn the piece as shown. Do not trim. Using a ¼" (6mm) seam, sew 2" (5.1cm) strips of white background fabric to the other sides. These strips should be at least 2½" (6.4cm) long. Press the seams away from the center.

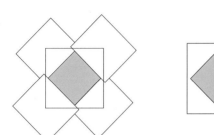

3. Trim each side ¼" (0.6cm) from the corner point. The diagram on the right shows the trimmed piece.

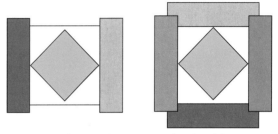

4. Add a round of colored strips to each side of the center section.

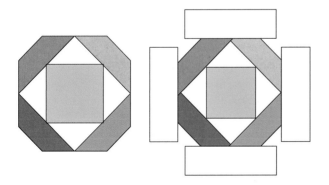

5. Trim, then add white strips.

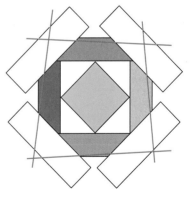

6. This time, trim at a slight angle. The red line in the photo shows crooked trimming lines. This begins the wonky part of these blocks.

7. Continue to alternate between adding colored strips and adding white strips and making angled trims. Once you have a total of four rounds of white strips and colored strips (ending with colored), sew on the white HSTs to fill out the last corners.

8. After making a few blocks, measure and trim to 10½" (26.7cm) square. If desired, make four blocks using a different background fabric.

Make forty-two blocks.

Quilt Assembly

Arrange the blocks into seven rows of six blocks. Place the four blocks with the different backgrounds together as shown in the diagram below or in any other position. Sew the blocks in each row together using a ¼″ (6mm) seam. Press. Sew the rows together using a ¼″ (6mm) seam. Press.

Finishing the Quilt
Borders

1. Remove selvages and sew the 3½″ (8.9cm) border strips into one long strip.

2. Measure the quilt from side to side and cut two border sections to this length. Sew the top and bottom borders in place with a ¼″ (6mm) seam. Press away from the center.

3. Measure the length of the quilt with the top and bottom borders on and cut two border pieces to this length. Sew the right and left borders in place with a ¼″ (6mm) seam. Press away from the center.

Backing, Quilting, and Binding

1. The backing piece should be at least 74″ x 84″ (188 x 213.4cm). Sew two 74″ (188cm) x WOF (42″ [106.7cm]) strips together as shown after trimming off the selvages. Press seam.

2. Layer the backing, batting, and quilt top together and baste. Quilt as desired.

3. Bind the quilt. See page 52 for binding instructions.

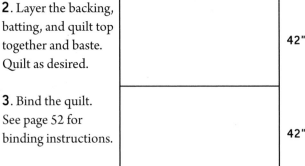

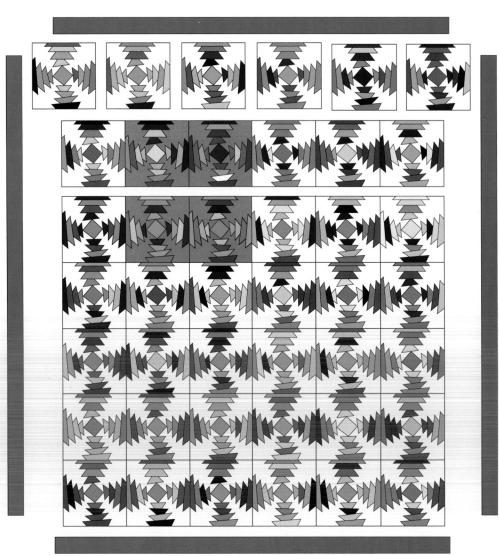

AROUND AND AROUND LOG CABIN

Use up leftover strips of fabric with this log cabin construction technique. Strips of varied lengths are sewn into long pieces, and these long pieces are then used for logs. The instructions are written for 2″ (5.1cm) strips, but the technique is easily adapted for strips of any size or even several sizes. See the Around and Around technique on page 42 for more information on using different-sized strips.

Vital Stats

Quilt size: 42″ x 54″ (106.7 x 137cm)
Block size: 12″ (30.5cm)
First border: ½″ (1.3cm)
Second border: 2″ (5.1cm)
Twelve blocks, four rows of three blocks

Quilted by **Yessant Habetz**

Tools and Materials

- Block centers: One fat quarter (18″ x 22″ [45.7 x 55.9cm]):
    Cut twelve 3½″ (8.9cm) squares for block centers
- Logs: about twelve ¼ yard (22.9cm) cuts of fabric:
    Cut 2″ (5.1cm) strips
- First border: ⅜ yards (34.3cm) turquoise fabric:
    Cut six 1″ (2.5cm) fabric x WOF (42″ [106.7cm]) pieces
- Second border: ½ yard (45.7cm) solid pink fabric:
    Cut six 2½″ (6.4) fabric x WOF (42″ [106.7cm]) strips
- Backing: 2½ yards (228.6cm):
    Cut two 50″ (127cm) x WOF (42″ [106.7cm]) pieces
- Binding: ½ yard (45.7cm):
    Cut six 2½″ (6.4cm) x WOF (42″ [106.7cm]) strips (or make scrappy binding)

Block Construction

1. Prepare a long length of log fabric as follows: Cut log fabric into 2″ (5.1cm) wide strips. Vary the length of the strips. From WOF (42″ [107cm]) strips, I cut off 15″ (38cm), 10″ (25cm), 6″ (15cm), and 5″ (13cm) pieces. Whatever is left is another piece. Sew the strips together into one very long strip (or several very long strips), varying the fabric and length of pieces.

2. Using a 3½″ (8.9cm) center, start using cuts from a long strip for logs. Place the first log, trim off any excess length, and join the log to one side of the center. Turn the block 90 degrees counterclockwise and trim. Use the long strip, starting where you cut the previous log, to cut and then apply logs in the same way around the other three sides of the center.

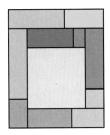

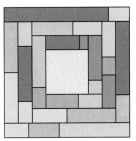

3. After completing the first round, continue in the same way. Rotate to the left, trim, continue using the same long pieced strip and add a new log. Press away from the center.

4. Keep going until you've completed all three rounds.

5. Trim all blocks to the same size. I trimmed these to 12½″ (31.8cm) so that they finished at 12″ (30.5cm).

Quilt Assembly

Quilt Center

Arrange the blocks into four rows of three blocks. Sew the blocks in each row together using a ¼″ (6mm) seam. Press. Sew the rows together using a ¼″ (6mm) seam. Press.

Borders

First Border

1. Remove selvages and sew the 1″ (2.5cm) border strips into one long strip.

2. Measure the quilt from side to side. Cut two border sections to this length. Sew the top and bottom borders in place with a ¼″ (6mm) seam. Press away from the center.

3. Measure the length of the quilt with the top and bottom borders on. Cut two border pieces to this length. Sew the right and left borders in place with a ¼″ (6mm) seam. Press away from the center.

Second Border

1. Remove the selvages and sew the 2½″ (6.4cm) border strips into one long strip.

2. Measure the quilt from side to side. Cut two border sections to this length. Sew the top and bottom borders in place with a ¼″ (6mm) seam. Press away from the center.

3. Measure the length of the quilt with the top and bottom borders on. Cut two border pieces to this length. Sew the right and left borders in place with a ¼″ (6mm) seam. Press away from the center.

Finishing the Quilt

1. The backing needs to measure 50″ x 62″ (127 x 157.5cm). Sew two 50″ (127cm) x WOF (42″ [106.7cm]) strips together as shown after trimming off the selvages. Press the seam open.

2. Layer the backing, batting, and quilt top together and baste. Quilt as desired.

3. Bind the quilt. See page 52 for binding instructions.

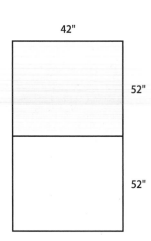

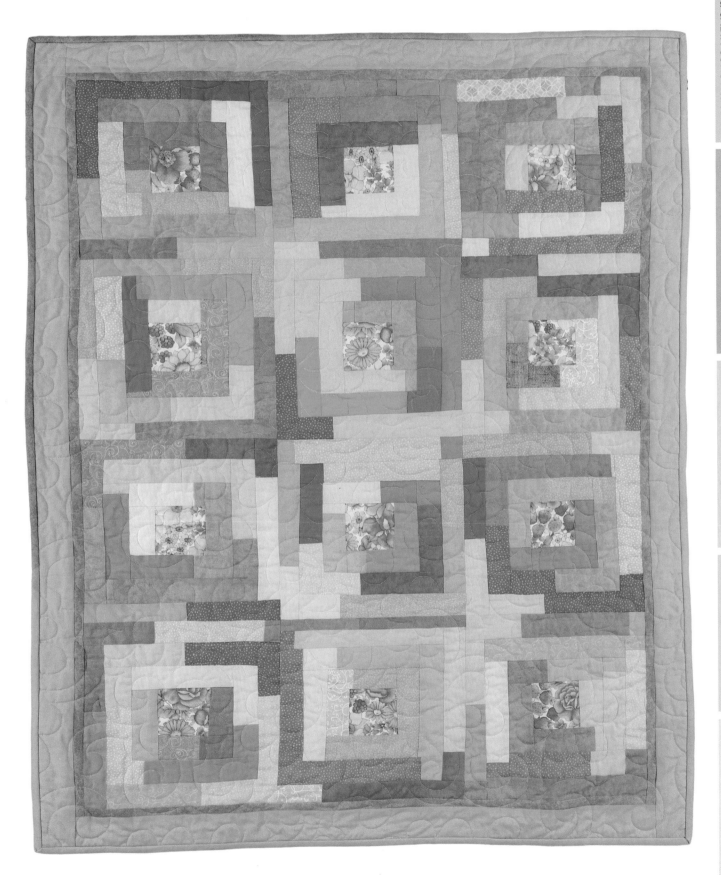

CIRCLE LOG CABIN

I'd like to acknowledge Nicholas Ball, because I first considered using circles for log cabin centers after reading his book *Inspiring Improv* (Lucky Spools, 2019), although my method is somewhat different. Here, I started with a 5″ (12.7cm) circle center and joined small logs around the center, then added larger logs to complete the block. This quilt was made with green and blue fabrics, yellow and red for the centers, and occasional bits of red, orange, and yellow. The location of the center circle within the block varies. I love the swirly look of these blocks.

Vital Stats

Quilt size: 44″ (111.8cm) square
Block size: 11″ (27.9cm) square
Sixteen blocks, four rows of four blocks

Quilted by **Yessant Habetz**

IMPROVISATION TIP

• Small pieces of contrasting fabric

Tools and Materials

• Cutting mat large enough to square up 11½″ (29.2cm) blocks
• Foundations: 12″ (30.5cm) square newsprint, drawing paper, parchment paper, or lightweight non-woven interfacing
• Yellow circle centers: One fat quarter or scraps:
   Cut twelve 5″ (12.7cm) circles, template on page 117
• Red circle centers: ¼ yard (22.9cm), one fat quarter, or scraps:
   Cut four 5″ (12.7cm) circles, template on page 117
• Logs: Assorted scrap fabrics in desired colors (Yardage is not provided because of the use of scrap fabrics.)
• Backing: 3 yards (274.3cm):
   Cut two 52″ (132.1cm) x WOF (42″ [106.7cm]) pieces
• Binding: ⅜ yard (34.3cm):
   Cut five 2½″ (6.4cm) x WOF (42″ [106.7cm]) strips (or make scrappy binding)

Block Construction

These blocks are more difficult than other log cabin blocks and benefit from a bit of practice. I recommend starting with a test block or two to work through the instructions and learn the basics. It is worth the effort because these blocks look so cool.

It is particularly challenging to keep circle log cabin blocks flat, as adding multiple logs at varying angles may lead to blocks that become mountains or bowls. Don't give up if you have difficulty with your first few blocks. Every seam should be straight.

I made the blocks at least 12″ (30.5cm) square, then trim to 11½″ (29.2cm) for a finished size of 11″ (27.9cm). (**Note:** The instructions show a block made from different fabrics than the blocks used in the project.)

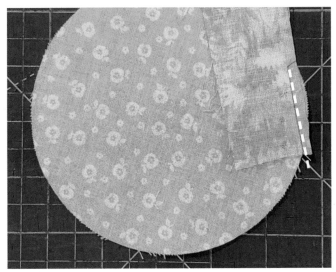

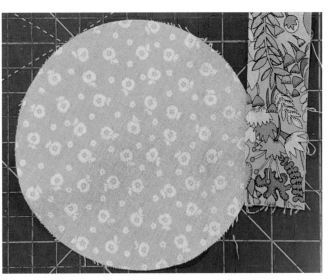

1. Cut eleven to thirteen 1½″ x 4″ (3.8 x 10.2cm) strips for the first round. Place a 1½″ (3.8cm) strip right side down on a circle close to the edge. Sew a scant ¼″ (6mm) from the edge of the fabric as shown. I used red thread and added a white dashed line to show where the log is sewn. The sewing should run off the edge. (**Note:** The last log of the first round will be tucked under the first log.)

2. Press carefully. Press the seam allowance with a fold, even where there is no sewing.

TIPS FOR FLAT BLOCKS

- Use a temporary paper foundation or a permanent foundation, for example, lightweight non-woven interfacing.
- Press well on both the front and back sides before adding a new log. Use starch or a starch alternative.
- A walking foot may help.
- Make sure each seam is straight. Correct crooked seams immediately after pressing, using the press lines as a guide.

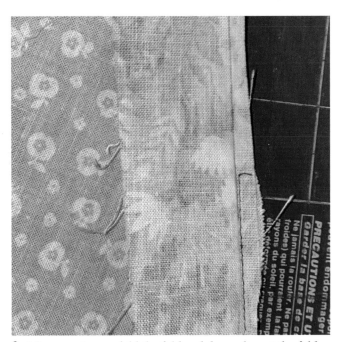

3. After pressing, unfold the fold and draw a line at the fold line with a pencil or marker. You will use this line later to sew the final strip of the first round.

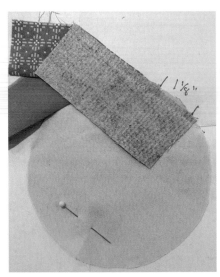

4. Place the second log at an angle so that it meets the edge of the previous log (note the circle) and covers part of the center edge as shown. I stitched in red to show where the log is sewn. The stitching runs off the edge (note the rectangle).The extra fabric to the right of this seam should be trimmed away.

5. The photo shows the seam pressed away from the center.

6. After adding each log, trim any fabric behind the new log. Each added log on this first round should cover about 1⅛″ to 1¼″ (2.9 to 3.2cm) of the circle's edge. After adding each log, trim any fabric behind the new log.

7. Continue adding new logs, trimming behind each log, and pressing before adding the next log.

8. Once you have sewn four strips to the center, pin the block-in-progress to a 12″ (30.5cm) foundation. It does not need to be centered exactly (unless you prefer it that way!).

9. Continue adding small logs in the same way: place them carefully, join them to the center circle, move the foundation out of the way and trim behind each new log, and press away from the center.

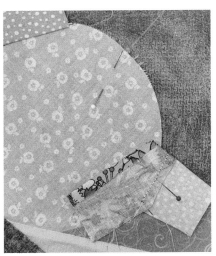

10. Once you are just several logs from reaching the starting point, turn back the first log and pin it out of the way. Continue to add logs but be mindful of spacing so that the last few logs will fit into place. Continue adding new logs, trimming behind each log, and pressing before adding the next log.

11. Place the last log of the first round carefully. It should just meet the edge under the first log and extend to the edge of the previous log. Sew into place, trim behind it, and press.

12. This is a bit fiddly, but it works if you do it this way. Unfold the first log and press it as if it is sewn into place.

13. Carefully unfold the first log without moving its position on top of the last log. Pin to keep it from moving. Sew along the line you drew in step 3. Trim behind the log and press. At this point, you've completed the first round! Rejoice! It will be easier next time.

14. Cut 2″ (5.1cm) strips for the rest of the logs. Start adding the second round of logs, continuing in the same general direction around the center and using the same process: add a log, trim behind the log, and press away from the center. (**Note:** You don't need to place these logs as precisely as the first round, but do not try to cover too much at one time.)

15. Continue adding 2″ (5.1cm) logs until the foundation is completely covered.

16. Mark the cutting lines on the block with a marker or pencil. Sew a straight line about ⅛″ (3mm) inside the drawn line for stay-stitching.

17. Trim the block to the correct size. A completed block is shown here.

Make sixteen blocks, four with red centers and the rest with yellow centers.

TROUBLESHOOTING

Adjusting Crooked Seams

- If a seam is not straight, it will be evident after you press it.

- Sew just to the right of the pressed line to straighten it.

- These photos show the stitching on the pressed line. Press the seam again after correcting it.

5" Circle template

TROUBLESHOOTING

Covering a Corner

- When finishing a block, you may find a small gap at the corner.

- Instead of adding just a tiny piece of fabric, add a larger piece. This makes the previous log narrower but provides more reasonable coverage of the corner.

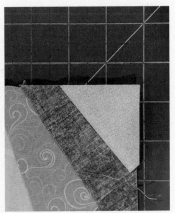

Quilt Assembly

Arrange the blocks into four rows of four blocks, as in the finished quilt photo. Sew the blocks in each row together using a ¼" (6mm) seam. Press. Sew the rows together using a ¼" (6mm) seam. Press.

Finishing the Quilt

1. The backing piece should be at least 52" (132.1cm) square. Sew two 52" (132.1cm) x WOF (42" [106.7cm]) pieces together as shown.

2. Layer the backing, batting, and quilt top together and baste. Quilt as desired.

3. Bind the quilt. See page 52 for binding instructions.

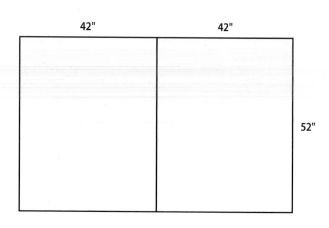

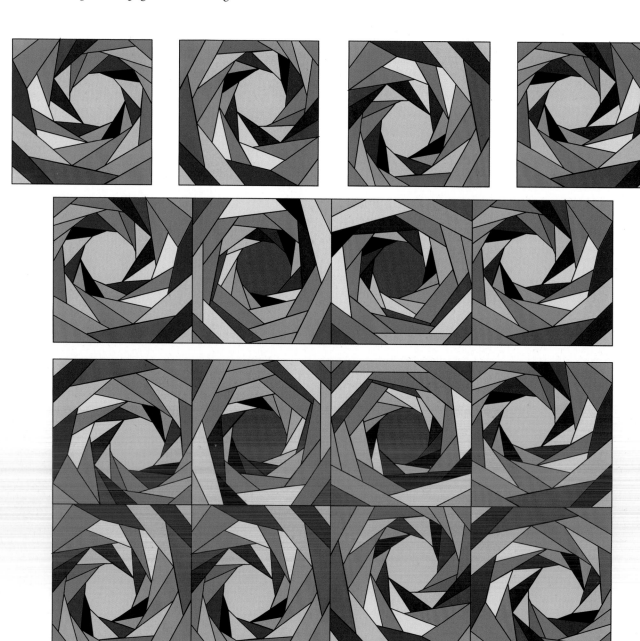

STACK, SLASH, SHUFFLE, AND SEW

This is a different approach to making log cabin blocks inspired by the work of Karla Alexander. I thought it would be fun to use this method, and I made the blocks in sets of four, using four fat quarters for each set of log cabins. Stack the fabric, cut it, shuffle the layers, and sew it back together to make four blocks at a time. The instructions are very detailed to clearly explain the block construction process.

The photo shows an example of four blocks made from four fat quarters. You can see a simpler version with just one round on page 44.

Vital Stats

Quilt size: 60″ (152cm) X 73″ (185cm)
Block size: 13″ (33.02 cm) square
First border: 1¼″ (3.2cm)
Second border: 2½″ (7cm)
Twenty blocks, 5 rows of 4 blocks

Quilted by **Kelly Borns**

Tools and Materials

- Cutting mat large enough to cut 18″ (45.7cm) squares (**Note:** Using a mat small enough to rotate will help when slashing [cutting] logs.)
- Blocks: Twenty fat quarters (five sets of four fat quarters), half light and half dark, or at least with noticeable contrast between the values in each set
- First border: ½ yard (45.7cm) orange fabric:
    Cut eight 1¾″ (4.5cm) x WOF (42″ [106.7cm]) strips
- Second border: Make string sets with either leftover fabric from the blocks, or a few additional fat quarters or scraps of coordinating fabric, or ¾ yard (68.6cm) fabric (**Note:** If you prefer not to make string sets, you can cut eight 3″ (7.6cm) x WOF (42″ [106.7cm]) strips for the second border.)
- Backing: 4 yards (366cm):
    Cut two 68″ (172.7cm) x WOF (42″ [106.7cm]) pieces
- Binding: ⅝ yard (57.1cm) green fabric:
    Cut eight 2½″ (6.4cm) x WOF (42″ [106.7cm]) strips (or make scrappy binding)

Block Construction

Stack

1. Stack four fat quarters in this order: dark, light, dark, light, making sure there is significant dark and light contrast within the groups of fabrics. (**Note:** Fat quarters are often not cut exactly, so there may be edges that don't match completely, but this is OK.)

2. Trim the fat quarters to about 18″ (45.7cm) square. Save any extra fabric for the second border. You will trim the blocks later.

Slash

1. Slash each stack of four fabrics using the instructions that follow. You will end up with four stacks of fabric: Centers, Round 1, Round 2, and Round 3. Make sure your rotary cutter blade is sharp so that you can make clean cuts through all the layers. Have paper and a pencil or pen handy so that you can label the sections.

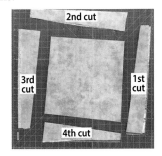

2. Cut Round 3 first as shown in the photo, using a slight angle for each cut. (**Note**: You cut the rounds in the reverse order of how you sew them.) Rotate the mat as you cut to make cutting more convenient. If you are left-handed, orient the block and cuts in the opposite way of the photo.

3. Cut Round 2 in the same way but leave the stacks from Round 3 where they are. Keep the angles of the segments the same as in the previous round as shown.

4. Cut Round 1 in the same way without moving the stacks from Rounds 2 and 3. Keep the angles of the segments the same as in the previous round as shown.

After cutting three sets of pieces all around.

Shuffle

1. Prepare labels for marking the stacks of fabric as follows:
Centers: Center 1, Center 2, Center 3, Center 4
Round 1: 1A, 1B, 1C, 1D
Round 2: 2A, 2B, 2C, 2D
Round 3: 3A, 3B, 3C, 3D
(**Note:** For me, adding labels was critical to keeping things in the correct order, and I highly recommend you do the same.)

2. Shuffle the stacks as follows:
Center: Move three pieces to the bottom of the stack
Round 1: Move two pieces to the bottom of each stack
Round 2: Move one piece to the bottom of each stack
Round 3: Do not shuffle any fabrics in the Round 3 stacks

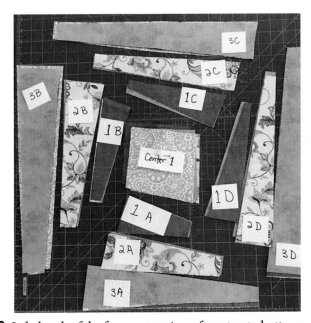

3. Label each of the four center pieces from top to bottom: Center 1, Center 2, Center 3, and Center 4.
Label the other stacks as shown.

Stack, Slash, Shuffle, and Sew **121**

Sew
Joining Round 1

1. Start by sewing the first round together. Shown here are the first-round pieces ready to sew.

2. Pick up and join the 1A pieces to the center for all four blocks using a ¼" (6mm) seam. Press away from the center piece. Put the joined pieces back in place, using the numbers on the centers to put them in the correct order.

3. Trim the edge straight, if needed, before joining the 1B logs. The stack shown is ready for the 1B logs.

4. The first log 1B is pinned and ready to sew.

5. Trim the edge of the center plus logs 1A and 1B before joining log 1C.

6. Trim the edge of the centers, plus logs 1A, 1B, and 1C before joining log 1D. The round is complete after you've added all 1D segments.

Joining Round 2

1. Continue in the same manner to join the second-round logs: Trim the A side of the block and then join log 2A. Press away from the center. Put the joined pieces back in place, using the numbers on the centers to put them in the correct order.

3. Trim the C side of the block and then join log 2C. Press away from the center. Put the joined pieces back in place, using the numbers on the centers to put them in the correct order.

2. Trim the B side of the block and then join log 2B. Press away from the center. Put the joined pieces back in place, using the numbers on the centers to put them in the correct order.

4. Trim the D side of the block and then join log 2D. Press away from the center. Put the joined pieces back in place, using the numbers on the centers to put them in the correct order.

Joining Round 3

1. Continue in the same manner to join the third-round logs. Trim the A side of the block and then join log 3A. Press away from the center. Put the joined pieces back in place, using the numbers on the centers to put them in the correct order.

2. Trim the B side of the block and then join log 3B. Press away from the center. Put the joined pieces back in place, using the numbers on the centers to put them in the correct order.

3. Trim the C side of the block and then join log 3C. Press away from the center. Put the joined pieces back in place, using the numbers on the centers to put them in the correct order.

4. Trim the D side of the block and then join log 3D. Press away from the center. Put the joined pieces back in place, using the numbers on the centers to put them in the correct order.

   Make a total of twenty blocks, making four blocks at a time. After making all twenty blocks, find the smallest block and trim all blocks to that size. I trimmed my blocks to 13½″ (34.3cm).

Quilt Assembly

Quilt Center

Arrange the blocks into five rows of four blocks. Sew the blocks in each row together using a ¼″ (6mm) seam. Press. Sew the rows together using a ¼″ (6mm) seam. Press.

Borders:
First Border

1. Remove the selvages and sew the 1¼″ (3.2cm) border strips into one long strip.

2. Measure the quilt from side to side. Cut two border sections to this length. Sew the top and bottom borders in place with a ¼″ (6mm) seam. Press away from the center.

3. Measure the length of the quilt with the top and bottom borders on. Cut two border pieces to this length. Sew the right and left borders in place with a ¼″ (6mm) seam. Press away from the center.

Completed and trimmed blocks from these fat quarters.

Second Border

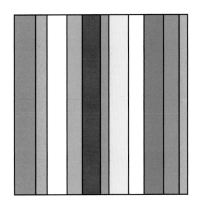

1. Use the fabric left from the twenty fat quarters for blocks. These will be about 3″ x 18″ (7.6 x 45.7cm). Cut 1″ to 2″ (2.5 to 5cm) x 18″ (45.7cm) strips. You will need additional strips of fabric to achieve the length needed for the border. Sew strips together lengthwise into strip sets that are about 10″ to 15″ (25.4 to 38.1cm) wide.

2. Cut into 3″ (7.6cm) segments, then sew these segments together end to end. Continue making strip sets, cutting 3″ (7.6cm) segments and sewing them together until you have at least 270″ (685.8cm) of 3″ (7.6cm) strip sets.

Stack, Slash, Shuffle, and Sew **123**

3. Measure the quilt from side to side. Cut two border sections to this length. Sew the top and bottom borders in place with a ¼″ (6mm) seam. Press toward the center.

4. Measure the length of the quilt with the top and bottom borders on. Cut two border pieces to this length. Sew the right and left borders in with a ¼″ (6mm) seam. Press toward the center.

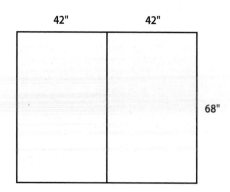

Finishing the Quilt

1. The backing piece should be at least 68″ x 81″ (172.7 x 205.7cm). Sew two 68″ (172.7cm) x WOF (42″ [106.7cm]) strips together as shown after trimming off the selvages. Press the seam.

2. Layer the backing, batting, and quilt top together and baste. Quilt as desired.

3. Bind the quilt. See page 52 for binding instructions.

Index

Note: Page numbers in *italics* indicate projects.

Photo Credits

Step-by-step photography and all other photos (unless otherwise stated) are by Mary M. Hogan

Studio photography by Mike Mihalo: 1, 2, 12 (bottom), 17 (bottom), 32 (top right, bottom right), 33 (top right), 35 (bottom), 47, 73, 77, 89, 93, 97, 111, 119

Additional photos by Ginger Liemohn: 8, 31 (top left), 53, 57, 61, 65, 69, 81, 84 (bottom left), 85, 103, 107, 125

Additional photos by Kimberly Fisk: 5, 6, 15, 29, 48

Shutterstock: MaxCab, 9 (top); ksakphoto, 9 (bottom); lev.studio, 10

Illustrations by Mary Ann Kahn

Acknowledgments

To Gwen Marston, whose book *Liberated Quiltmaking* gave me permission to do things my way

To Karla Alexander, whose books showed me how to stack, slash, shuffle, and sew

To Kathy Schmidt, for showing me curve basics

To Dianne Hire, for the ⅛″ seams

To Kathleen Loomis, for coaching on fine lines

To Nicolas Ball, whose book inspired me to develop circle log cabins

And especially:
To George, for our extraordinary life together, also for the coffee

About the Author

Mary has dabbled with fabric and sewing since she started making handmade doll clothes as a child, quickly progressing to using a sewing machine to make clothes, stuffed toys, and dolls. She also began quilting nearly thirty years ago, and, now retired from a career in nursing and healthcare, she gladly spends as much time as possible quilting.

A few years into quilting, Mary decided to stop following instructions, and she found that she liked it better that way! She usually starts a quilt by picking out the fabric and then letting the quilt evolve as she's making it. Scrappy quilts with a lot of fabric make her happy. She now follows only one rule: don't leave the rotary cutter open!

Passionate about helping quilters value themselves and their work, she loves coaching and teaching. She sees her books as a way to provide support to quilters everywhere, and her motto is "Trust yourself, enjoy what you do, make quilts."

Mary earned her BS in nursing from Loyola University, Chicago; her MS in public health nursing from the University of Illinois at Chicago; and her PhD in health service research from the University of Michigan at Ann Arbor. She grew up in Illinois in a large family and now lives in Michigan with her husband in a house overflowing with fabric, thread, quilts, sewing machines, and kindness.